T0326358

Cambridge Elements ≡

Elements in Quantitative and Computational Methods
for the Social Sciences
edited by
R. Michael Alvarez
California Institute of Technology
Nathaniel Beck
New York University
Betsy Sinclair
Washington University in St. Louis

EXTERNAL VALIDITY AND EVIDENCE ACCUMULATION

Tara Slough
New York University

Scott A. Tyson
University of Rochester

Shaftesbury Road, Cambridge CB2 8EA, United Kingdom

One Liberty Plaza, 20th Floor, New York, NY 10006, USA

477 Williamstown Road, Port Melbourne, VIC 3207, Australia

314–321, 3rd Floor, Plot 3, Splendor Forum, Jasola District Centre,
New Delhi – 110025, India

103 Penang Road, #05–06/07, Visioncrest Commercial, Singapore 238467

Cambridge University Press is part of Cambridge University Press & Assessment,
a department of the University of Cambridge.

We share the University's mission to contribute to society through the pursuit of
education, learning and research at the highest international levels of excellence.

www.cambridge.org
Information on this title: www.cambridge.org/9781009486033

DOI: 10.1017/9781009375856

When citing this work, please include a reference to the DOI 10.1017/9781009375856

First published 2024

A catalogue record for this publication is available from the British Library

ISBN 978-1-009-48603-3 Hardback
ISBN 978-1-009-37581-8 Paperback
ISSN 2398-4023 (online)
ISSN 2514-3794 (print)

External Validity and Evidence Accumulation

Elements in Quantitative and Computational Methods for the Social Sciences

DOI: 10.1017/9781009375856
First published online: December 2024

Tara Slough
New York University

Scott A. Tyson
University of Rochester

Author for correspondence: Scott A. Tyson, styson2@ur.rochester.edu

Abstract: The accumulation of empirical evidence that has been collected in multiple contexts, places, and times requires a more comprehensive understanding of empirical research than is typically required for interpreting the findings from individual studies. The authors advance a novel conceptual framework where causal mechanisms are central to characterizing social phenomena that transcend context, place, or time. They distinguish various concepts of external validity, all of which characterize the relationship between the effects produced by mechanisms in different settings. Approaches to evidence accumulation require careful consideration of cross-study features, including theoretical considerations that link constituent studies and measurement considerations about how phenomena are quantified. The authors' main theoretical contribution is developing *uniting principles* that constitute the qualitative and quantitative assumptions that form the basis for a quantitative relationship between constituent studies. The authors then apply their framework to three approaches to studying general social phenomena: meta-analysis, replication, and extrapolation.

Keywords: external validity, replication, meta-analysis, measurement, target-equivalence

JEL classifications: C18, C81, C82, C90

ISBNs: 9781009486033 (HB), 9781009375818 (PB), 9781009375856 (OC)
ISSNs: 2398-4023 (online), 2514-3794 (print)

Contents

1 Introduction

The social sciences advance through concept development and empirical inquiry. Dominant approaches in every branch of the social sciences have become increasingly quantified, both in the way theories are expressed and the empirical tools employed. These developments have led to marked improvements in understanding social phenomena, some of which have been adopted by policymakers who use these quantitative findings to shape individual incentives and institutions.[1] Given the increasing centrality of quantitative empirical research in the social sciences, it is important to know what is learned or what kind of knowledge is acquired from the collection of quantitative empirical research in the social sciences.

The goal of empirical social science must be to isolate and understand the substantive forces that transcend the idiosyncrasies of time, place, and circumstance. Otherwise, empirical research would be constrained to questions of historical description, and quantitative approaches would simply describe features of a sample taken from a snapshot of one setting. Is describing features of a sample the central aim of quantitative empirical social science? If it were, then knowing whether features of a sample generalize would not be a central concern. Questions of generalizability, mechanisms, evidence accumulation, and external validity invoke a concern with something beyond the description of a historical case or sample. Such questions *belie* an interest in features of the world that transcend individual circumstance. Moreover, they invoke the belief that empirical evidence about related phenomena – collected in different places and times – should be related.

Evaluating evidence that has been collected in multiple places and times, to gain broad general knowledge of social phenomena must be a central concern of the social sciences. Some practitioners as well as consumers of social science further seek to use their understanding of general social phenomena to shape the political and economic institutions that affect people's lives. Clarifying how empirical findings from one setting speak to more general phenomena is crucially important when empirical findings from one setting are used to inform policy at a later time or in a different place.

The broad goals of social science highlight the importance of observing a phenomenon beyond the confines of a single study. But doing so empirically does not follow straightforwardly from existing methods. The **accumulation of evidence** is the process of collecting and evaluating empirical findings from different places and times to discover whether these findings speak to a broader social phenomenon. Through this process, researchers can build a case

---

[1] See Hamming (1980) for similar argument applied to the sciences broadly.

about whether a general social phenomenon exists and learn about the properties of that phenomenon. Put simply, evidence accumulation is about making empirical findings *more than the sum of their parts*.

We organize this Element into two parts. The first part – Concepts – consists of three chapters that discuss the philosophical and conceptual underpinnings of external validity and evidence accumulation. The second part – Applications – applies the concepts developed in the first part to three research designs for evidence accumulation that are common in the literature.

1.1 Empiricism and Social Science

The social sciences are conceptually organized around the idea (or belief) that general substantive forces drive human decisions and behavior. How is knowledge about general social phenomena acquired? This Element proceeds under the supposition that experience and observation ultimately serve to test, develop, and correct social scientists' understanding of social phenomena, as well as the views held by other practitioners and consumers of social science.

The phenomena that social scientists aim to describe, characterize, and understand are held to be features of the world that are external to, or exist independently of, how those features are described by social scientists. Consequently, it is important to distinguish the domain of social scientific inquiry – the **external world** – from the malleable representations of that world used by the social scientists who study it.

Empiricism refers to a collection of philosophical ideas that are united by the commitment that knowledge about the external world emerges from observation and experience. When applied to social science, experience includes the elucidation and measurement of general behavioral forces and the observable phenomena they produce. In particular, modern quantitative social science aims to understand the external world through measurement and quantitative assessment. Uncovering the underlying structure of the external world, however, is not straightforward, especially when approached quantitatively.

The kind of knowledge that is gained through experience and observation is not always direct, and the aspects of the external world that are of the greatest interest often remain hidden from direct engagement or manipulation. Consequently, the substantive conclusions that are central to progress in the social sciences require an inference from experience. However, since forces in the external world remain hidden from direct view, inference from experience is subject to the well-known skeptic's objection that "[E]xperience only teaches us, how one event constantly follows another, without instructing us in the secret connexion, which binds them together and renders them inseparable" (Hume, 1777, p. 77). Skepticism about empirical knowledge that was motivated by this critique accelerated in the seventeenth century because there were not (and are not) simple answers to it (Dear, 1995, Ch. 1). Overcoming the skeptic's objection requires **methodology**, which consists of both the theoretical considerations to elucidate the "secret connexion" underlying experience, and the tools and practices needed to help uncover it (Diaconis & Skyrms, 2017).

Perhaps the most important methodological innovation developed in response to skepticism was *experimentalism*, which refers to a philosophical and conceptual framework for designating and characterizing knowledge. In particular, information about the external world, that was obtained through careful construction and analysis of an experiment, came to define knowledge about the external world (Mill, 1856). This conceptual innovation, in conjunction with important methodological developments (e.g., randomization), has had a profound impact in the natural and social sciences. Most recently, the philosophical views of experimentalism are reflected in the **credibility revolution** in the social sciences.

1.2 Experimentalism and the Credibility Revolution

Adhering more closely to an experimentalist formulation of knowledge reflects a more serious attempt to answer skeptical criticisms of empirical social science. The goal of most empirical approaches in the social sciences has been to link empirical findings to a "mechanism," and it is the credibility of this link that comes under the most methodological scrutiny. An intellectual movement, typically referred to as the *credibility or identification revolution*, constitutes a philosophical/theoretical position that is characterized by specific goals and methodological aesthetics. These goals can be summarized by three guiding principles:

1. *A model of causality*: Causality is defined within the potential outcomes model.
2. *Methodological commitments*: Identification arises from a model of a research design rather than a model of the data-generating process.
3. *Evaluating estimators*: Unbiasedness is prioritized over other properties of estimators.

The credibility revolution represents a shift in the attention of empirical scholars toward design-based methods, where identification rests on the model of the research design, rather than alternatives where identification rests on specifying an elaborate model of the external world (e.g., Angrist & Pischke, 2010; Banerjee & Duflo, 2009; Imbens & Wooldridge, 2009; Samii, 2016).

Methodological tools associated with the credibility revolution were largely developed in the medical sciences in response to fears that the heavy reliance on elaborate biological models could expose patients to unnecessary harms in medical research, and in particular, drug trials. Medical research that is less reliant on elaborate models is thus thought to provide patients with stronger protections. Expressing similar concerns, Aronow and Miller (2019) describe the credibility revolution's reduced reliance on statistical models as stemming from "a growing acknowledgment that the evidence that researchers adduce for their claims is often predicated on unsustainable assumptions" (p. xv). The embrace of more "agnostic" methods stems from concerns that models of the external world, when misspecified, produce inferences that are wildly misleading. Moreover, when research is used to inform policy, recommendations taken from fallacious models could be harmful.

Design-based strategies aim to ensure that certain important identifying assumptions are plausible by virtue of a study's research design. Proponents of the credibility revolution advise being explicit about the assumptions that a study invokes to support both *identification* and *estimation* of treatment effects, and whenever possible, a link between these assumptions and the research designs employed. It is important to emphasize that designed-based strategies do not limit the need for *any* model of the external world, nor do they necessarily render *every* assumption reasonable. Instead, design-based strategies rely more heavily on a model of a research design with a reduced reliance on a model of the external world (whenever possible).

Aside from concerns about identification, a distinct and equally important part of any empirical study involves estimation. When assessing an estimator, proponents of the credibility revolution have generally stressed the importance of *statistical unbiasedness*. Approaches developed in the credibility revolution put substantial (if not exclusive) weight on unbiasedness as the objective when selecting or evaluating an estimator. Unbiasedness of an estimator is about what the statistical measure in a study "aims at."

1.3 The Accumulation of Knowledge

Whether evidence about a particular phenomenon, collected in one place or time, is instructive about that phenomenon in other places/times is ultimately a question about **external validity**. In this Element, we precisely articulate and organize different concepts of external validity. In uncovering these distinct concepts, we identify empirical approaches that are consistent with the principles that have guided the credibility revolution (articulated in the previous section).

We show that popular approaches to problems of external validity, generalization, and evidence accumulation cannot ensure – and sometimes contradict – key principles of the credibility revolution. By identifying these tensions, we highlight how learning about external validity requires *building on* the advances of the credibility revolution and careful engagement with research design. We outline different approaches to external validity and evidence accumulation, emphasizing the conditions under which empirical findings can be given a quantitative and a causal interpretation. Our discussion is therefore largely theoretical, and focuses on the conceptual foundations of external validity and evidence accumulation, rather than statistical features, which can often mask deeper issues.

Applied to experiments, external validity answers common critiques related to the findings from randomized-controlled trials (RCTs). For instance, Deaton (2010, p. 448) argues that "for an RCT to produce 'useful knowledge' beyond its local context, it must illustrate some general tendency, some effect that is the result of a mechanism that is likely to apply more broadly." This point is correct and the logic is straightforward. In the absence of common mechanisms that might produce similar treatment effects in multiple places, it is unclear why an internally valid estimate in one setting should provide *any* information about the analogous effect of the treatment in another setting. However, this critique has little to do with experiments, and by extension RCTs, because it applies to any empirical study. It indirectly points to the critical importance of evidence accumulation, which is *the only empirical answer to questions about general social phenomena*.

We stress that external validity is a property of a substantive phenomenon, such as a mechanism, rather than a single empirical finding. The heavy reliance on design-based methods for causal inference often leads to the selection of settings and research designs for convenience reasons. Consequently, the design-based perspective can lead researchers to focus on a part of a sample that is not representative, and hence leaves unanswered questions of whether the conclusions drawn from a convenience sample apply more broadly. This strategy, however, does not clearly reflect the kind of "reliability of manipulation" normally associated with external validity. Specifically, efforts to restrict a sample serve to isolate an effect from mitigating factors, whose influence is harder to discern. It is a study's "empirical target" that needs to apply beyond the confines of the individual study setting and not any specific finding per se.

PART I: CONCEPTS

The accumulation of empirical evidence across multiple contexts requires a more comprehensive view of the empirical enterprise than is usually needed for single studies. In particular, the accumulation of evidence requires an understanding of what ties different studies together and how important context is to research design. We emphasize that these considerations include both theoretical features that link constituent studies to more general phenomena, and measurement choices about how phenomena are quantified in each context.

In the first part of this Element, we develop concepts that facilitate evaluation of various approaches to evidence accumulation. We start by considering what aspects of mechanisms matter for the accumulation of evidence. We focus first on how mechanisms are defined and how their effects are measured. We then present a novel theoretical account of measurement. Second, we survey and provide a new classification of various formulations of external validity that are used by empirical scholars. Finally, we develop a new concept for evidence accumulation, **uniting principles**, which provide the foundation of any effort to combine, assess, or synthesize evidence across studies. Uniting principles are the set of arguments and models that relate studies both qualitatively and quantitatively. Different forms of uniting principles are invoked in existing efforts to accumulate evidence, but these considerations are rarely acknowledged explicitly.

In this part, we present four key takeaways:

1. An interest in general social phenomena belies an interest in mechanisms.
2. When studying a mechanism empirically, it is critical to consider how its influence is measured.
3. Any empirical approach that assesses the generality of social phenomena necessarily engages with some form of external validity.
4. Any approach to evidence accumulation must articulate uniting principles, which characterize relationships between studies. Quantitative approaches require quantitative uniting principles.

2 Measurement

The central goal of evidence accumulation is to discover whether empirical findings, collected in one particular place and time, speak to a broader social phenomenon. A critical part of this process relies on concept formation, which involves defining, representing, and characterizing a phenomenon so that questions of measuring it can be answered with the theory, data, and methods that are available to the researcher. Importantly, the processes of concept formation and measurement are not exclusively empirical or methodological.

The objective of quantitative empirical studies is to make inferences about substantive phenomena—to extract the signal from the noise—quantitatively, thus providing a measure of some feature of the external world.[2] But many attributes of an empirical study, such as sampling and the realization

---

[2] This view was originally formulated by Venn (1888).

of treatment assignment, ineluctably introduce randomness into the data. Consequently, idiosyncratic error that is orthogonal to the social phenomenon of interest is always present in the data to some degree or another. None of these features – sampling into an experiment, random assignment, or data processing – are inherent to the phenomena of interest (by construction). Therefore, a single set of data provides one snapshot of the external world, and a different dataset provides a potentially very different snapshot. What makes these snapshots differ, and are there patterns in the ways they differ?

When thinking about the processes involved in measuring the external world, it is important to keep in mind that "data are typically the result of complex interactions among a large number of disparate causal factors which are idiosyncratic to a particular experimental situation" (Bogen & Woodward, 1988, p. 319). An important component of these interactions is the process of measuring empirical phenomena, which involves researcher ingenuity as well as the technological (and ethical) constraints the researcher confronts. In this section, we think about the importance of conceptual development and articulation in quantitative measurement of empirical phenomena.

2.1 Mechanisms

Thinking about general social phenomena involves a conceptual and ontological framework in which something can – and does – arise in seemingly disparate scenarios, and in ways that are somehow related. An interest in the underlying processes that govern general social phenomena – beyond immediate circumstances – thus belies an interest in what "entities and activities," or **mechanisms**, produce them. These mechanisms, which may be expected to arise in many places and times, are the central concern of the social sciences.

The idea that mechanisms are responsible for phenomena originates with a compelling analogy that the external world operates similar to a machine (Leibniz, 1714; Marquis de Laplace, 1825). Modern formulations of the mechanistic worldview take this analogy less literally, but retain the view that mechanisms are the parts of a complex system that underlie and produce observed phenomena and behavior in accordance with direct causal laws (Glennan, 1996, 2017). Mechanisms are therefore about the ontology of the "causal structure of the external world," and hence constitute part of the external world.

A *causal mechanism* is one type of mechanism that reliably produces a phenomenon in a special way (Woodward, 2002). They capture the core idea that "*if you perform such and such action, you will have such and such experiences*," or more generally, "*if anyone performs such and such actions, then such and such publicly observable events will take place*" (Putnam, 1981, pp. 180–182). Causal mechanisms are key conceptual ingredients in the social sciences because a single mechanism is held responsible for reliably producing a similar phenomenon in different places. A central tenet of the social sciences is that such mechanisms exist, and, if characterized precisely enough, they reliably and repeatedly produce the same phenomena.

2.2 A Theory of Measurement

Mechanisms are not directly observed, and hence their influence in the external world needs to be uncovered. The process of uncovering a mechanism's influence typically proceeds by setting up conditions where the mechanism can be activated *in isolation*, that is, without simultaneously activating other mechanisms or mitigating factors.[3] In doing so, the mechanism should reliably produce a similar influence. By positing a common mechanism (or a common bundle of mechanisms) as the feature of the external world that justifies evidence accumulation, we must take a broader perspective on measurement than that commonly presented in methodological texts.

It is important to keep distinct a mechanism's *influence*, which is how the mechanism manifests in the external world, from its *effect*, which is the measured (usually quantitative) object that is (or can be) observed. But a mechanism can be probed in different ways. Ultimately, because we seek to measure the influence of mechanisms through the effects that they produce, we must understand how those effects are created and quantified. For example, distinct manipulations – like varying dosages of a treatment – can activate a mechanism in different ways, leading to distinct measured effects. Furthermore, mechanisms typically influence multiple outcomes and their measured effect on one outcome may be very different from their measured effect on another outcome.

2.2.1 Conventional Views of Measurement

Conventional conceptions of measurement emerge from *scientific realism*, which holds that the theoretical objects of study are real and describe the external world literally (Chakravartty, 2007, pp. 8–13). A popular manifestation of this view in the social sciences is that (1) the analyst passively observes social phenomena (perhaps with noise), and (2) variables exist as quantities. Under these premises, a mechanism's influence is then simply a latent variable. The observed phenomenon – such as an observed causal effect – captures this latent variable, perhaps with some noise (Blair et al., 2019). Although there

---

[3] This says nothing about the practicality of such isolated activation.

is substantial variation in practice, these views are unified in their "God's Eye" perspective, where some abstract "true effect" determines a mechanism's influence across various settings.

Most methodological texts omit discussion (and often recognition) of the external world, and implicitly equate the external world with data, as though data were the object of study. Then, since data are equated with the relevant parts of the external world, they can essentially be passively gathered by researchers (e.g., Borsboom, 2005). This *naïve realist* view, that the external world presents variables as they are, and that humans perceive these variables (or data) directly, begs the question of an underlying quantitative structure to the external world that is independent of measurement. It thus reflects a metaphysical commitment that the quantitative concepts used by empirical social scientists, and the objects they represent in the external world, are the same and part of direct experience.

Conventional accounts of measurement often emphasize *construct validity*, which describes the relationship between an empirical measure and the theoretical construct it is meant to represent (Shadish et al., 2002). A measure is said to have good construct validity when it aligns closely with the theoretical construct it measures. Construct validity, however, implicitly requires that the theoretical construct, and the external world object it represents, be the same. That is, that there is no mismatch between a concept and what that concept represents in the external world.

Empirical measures are imperfect representations of both theoretical constructs and external world objects (e.g., mechanisms). It is important to emphasize that external world objects may differ from the theoretical constructs that represent them. Since any actual empirical measure is influenced by the external world object it judges and the theoretical construct used to create it, construct validity (as it is normally defined) necessarily reflects all the differences between the external world object and the theoretical construct it is meant to represent. Conventional presentations of construct validity neglect this difference, thereby presuming a closer connection between such constructs and the real causal structure of the external world than may be available. More fundamentally, the external world may, in fact, be less structured than such measurement exercises presume, thus leading to an over-reliance of empirical measures on the structure of conceptual representations. This problem afflicts evidence accumulation efforts acutely.

2.2.2 Measurement Perspectivism

Since the accumulation of evidence involves looking at studies conducted in different places/times, where so few things are held fixed, the metaphysical ambivalence common in empirical practice is misguided. Evidence accumulation requires a broader concept of measurement than what is typically supplied in conventional methodological texts. Our theory of measurement makes three central departures from canonical formulations of measurement. These departures identify why conventional accounts of measurement are incomplete. In particular, the position that a mechanism has an influence that is independent of measurement/comparison – like a latent variable – presumes facts about the external world, perception, and the technology of measurement that are not only strong, but also ultimately unknowable.

Our first departure from conventional accounts of measurement starts with the recognition that empirical observation necessarily occurs through the "lens" of how phenomena are conceptualized, measured, and, when relevant, quantified. The measurement of empirical phenomena in scientific practice thus plays a similar role to perception in individual knowledge – especially when applied to *quantitative knowledge*. How outcomes are measured, or what comparisons are made between a control and treatment group, all impact the quantitative measure of a mechanism's influence. Critically, when outcomes are measured differently, or when a different control/treatment contrast is evaluated, then a mechanism's measured effect is liable to be different.

We advocate for an alternative viewpoint, **measurement perspectivism**, which emphasizes that substantive phenomena are distinct from the tools we use to observe and measure them. Measurement perspectivism builds upon the broader notion of scientific perspectivism (Giere, 2010). While the distinction between scientific realism and perspectivism is largely irrelevant when focusing on individual studies, it is essential for understanding the relationship between disparate findings about the same mechanism. Measurement perspectivism holds that a measured effect is different when it is measured differently. Thus, distinguishing between how we measure the world, and what is ultimately "seen" in these measures, is a critical task when accumulating evidence.

Our second departure from conventional treatments of measurement is that our framework reflects a (potentially) less structured external world. We do not presume that the external world is comprised of variables, or that those variables need be quantities. Our position is simply that we could not know if the external world has such convenient features because we do not observe the external world directly (i.e., absent measurement). Our theory of measurement is thus more agnostic and can accommodate common assumptions about the external world, but it does not require them. Instead, we conceive of measurement strategies as providing a "scaffolding" that is erected onto the external world, thereby serving as a lens into the mechanisms and phenomena under study.

Third, we argue that measurement and observation are activities rather than merely a passive exercise. Researchers make choices about what concepts to measure, how to observe those measures, and how to quantify those observations. Each of these choices are actions that require individual judgment. Sometimes researchers rely on existing data like administrative data collected by governments, or surveys that have been conducted by other scholars or organizations. But using existing data simply means that a researcher relies on the choices made by others (Jerven, 2013). For example, bureaucrats typically determine the content of administrative data and policymaking politicians or bureaucrats examine how it is observed/used. The vast variation in the content, quantity, and quality of administrative data points to the importance of these choices (Schedler, 2012).

Treating measurement as an active, rather than a passive, process emphasizes that scholars choose the lens through which they aim to extract information about the external world. Using a different lens – by choosing different measurement strategies – means that different features of the data are produced and observed. Consider, for example, the information that is obtained through a survey. It is straightforward to see that asking a survey question in different ways, or providing a different response scale, is likely to produce different measures of an attitude or belief. While some might argue that physical or material phenomena are not subject to these considerations, the quantification of such physical or material phenomena depends on the instruments used for measurement, even in seemingly straightforward cases like temperature (Chang, 2001, 2004).

A key point of how measurement perspectivism departs from conventional accounts is that the measured effect of a mechanism will depend on how that mechanism is probed and how its influence is evaluated. Thus, no single treatment or outcome measure gives the "true effect" of a mechanism because no such effect exists. To be clear, our point is *not* that it is impossible to measure a mechanism's true effect – our position is that *no such effect exists*. Put differently, it does not make sense to talk of quantitative objects that are not dependent in some way on how they are defined and measured, since *measurement is precisely what transforms a mechanism's influence into a quantitative effect*.

2.3 Empirical Targets

Our theory of measurement stresses the importance of how the influence of a mechanism is conceptualized, quantified, and assessed. For a single study, these considerations culminate in the **empirical target**, which is the theoretical representation of the quantitative effect of a mechanism, under a specific research design and setting. The empirical target is what an empirical study aims to identify because it is the quantitative object that (ideally) connects with a mechanism's influence (Slough & Tyson, 2023, 2024). For example, causal research designs seek to identify the influence of a causal mechanism, and the empirical target serves as the measure of its effect.

Empirical targets depend on at least three critical ingredients of a *constituent study*. First, a study takes place in a *setting*, represented by $\theta \in \Theta$, and captures all the contextual features, as well as characteristics of the study population, that determine the mechanism's effect, or quantitative influence. The setting can include both measured and unmeasured features or characteristics that are relevant to how the mechanism's influence arises and how it is measured.

Second, every constituent study is associated with a specific research design, which is comprised of a comparison of interest and a set of quantitative measures. The quantitative effect of a mechanism involves a comparison, or *contrast*, formally represented by $(\omega', \omega'') \in C$. In an experiment, the contrast is defined through the choice of experimental conditions. In nonexperimental research, the contrast gives the comparison of interest, for example, comparing a new policy to the status quo. The other key part of a research design is its *measurement strategy*, formally represented by $m \in M$, which captures all the considerations researchers choose in order to observe and measure a mechanism's influence. These considerations include the measurement of both the contrast and the outcome of interest.

These three ingredients of a study, alone, do not provide sufficient information to measure a mechanism's influence because there exist many possible measures of a mechanism's influence within any given study. Researchers typically select an estimand to quantify the effect of a mechanism, generally through aggregation over units. A given measurement strategy and contrast can be evaluated with many different estimands, many of which may be related (e.g., Heckman & Vytlacil, 2005). For example, one might measure the effect of a mechanism through the average treatment effect or the quantile treatment effect evaluated at the median. These measures can, and typically do, yield different estimates of a mechanism's influence. We denote the estimand by γ, since this essential part of measurement serves to quantify a mechanism's influence in a specific way.[4]

---

[4] One could fold the estimand into the measurement strategy, but because researchers can adopt different estimands ex post, we separate it for clarity.

EMPIRICAL TARGET

For a constituent study $\mathcal{E} = \{m, (\omega', \omega''), \theta\}$, with research design, m, and contrast, (ω', ω''), the *empirical target* in setting θ, evaluated with estimand γ, is the treatment effect function:

$$\tau_m^\gamma(\omega', \omega'' \mid \theta). \tag{1}$$

A necessary step in providing any substantive quantitative explanation of a social phenomenon involves articulating and identifying empirical targets. In general, the empirical target, that is, the function, $\tau_m^\gamma(\omega', \omega'' \mid \theta)$, changes with aspects of a study's research design. Multiple interventions can activate the same mechanism, but a mechanism is liable to produce a different effect when activated differently.

For instance, consider the effect of insulin on blood sugar. There are two prominent ways of measuring blood sugar, either by a finger-stick blood sample or by a sample of interstitial fluid (the fluid between blood vessels and cells). Ascertaining the effect of insulin depends on a number of factors, including the type of insulin used. The two most prominent types of fast-acting insulin are insulin lispro (e.g., Humalog, Admelog) and regular insulin (e.g., Humulin R, Novolin R). First, a study comparing a 5 ml dose of insulin lispro to a 10 ml dose of insulin lispro will produce a different reduction in blood sugar than a study comparing a 5 ml dose to a 15 ml dose. Similarly, insulin lispro does not have the same effect on the reduction of blood sugar, measured using a finger-stick sample, as on blood sugar measured with interstitial fluid, and moreover, the gap between these two measures of insulin's effect depends on an individual's blood sugar at the time that insulin is injected. Finally, the reduction in blood sugar depends on whether the subject was injected with insulin lispro, regular insulin, or another longer lasting insulin. This discussion highlights how changes in a research design change the empirical target, which means that the treatment effect evaluated with an observed outcome also changes. Put formally, the treatment effect function, $\tau_m^\gamma(\omega', \omega'' \mid \theta)$, is not generically constant in contrasts, (ω'', ω'), and measurement strategies, m.

Since the empirical target is a mapping, $\tau_m^\gamma(\omega', \omega'' \mid \theta): M \times C \times \Theta \rightarrow \mathbb{R}$, many aspects of research design, that is, scope conditions, are captured by the domain of the empirical target, $M \times C \times \Theta$. For instance, the set of settings, Θ, is the set of all settings where the mechanism represented by τ can arise. If there is a setting where the mechanism could not arise, then that setting would not be in Θ. Similarly, the set of measurement strategies, M, and contrasts, C, include all of the possible ways of activating the mechanism (quantitatively) and measuring its effect. It is important to emphasize that the domain of the empirical target is often up to the discretion of the researcher to specify, and in more developed cases may be of separate interest to measure and study.

2.4 Meta-studies and Harmonization

By defining an empirical target precisely, and considering its ingredients explicitly, we can see how measurement influences the measured effect of a mechanism. While these considerations are important for the interpretation of empirical findings in constituent studies, they become essential when considering the effect of a common mechanism in different settings. In our framework, a *meta-study* is a collection of $N > 1$ studies:

$$\{\mathcal{E}_i = (m_i, (\omega'_i, \omega''_i), \theta_i)\}_{i=1}^N.$$

In particular, a meta-study is a collection of measurement strategies, contrasts, and settings – one for each constituent study.[5]

Our discussion above highlights how empirical targets can vary – even within setting – when a mechanism is evaluated using different contrasts or measurement strategies. It is therefore important to separate conceptually what leads to differences in empirical targets within the cross-study environment in any meta-study. To this end, we introduce *harmonization*, as a feature of multi-study research design that eliminates differences that emerge as artifacts of study design from different contrasts or measurement strategies.

HARMONIZATION

For a meta-study, $\{\mathcal{E}_i = (m_i, (\omega'_i, \omega''_i), \theta_i)\}_{i=1}^N$ two studies, i and j are

1. *measurement harmonized* if $m_i = m_j$;
2. *contrast harmonized* if $(\omega'_i, \omega''_i) = (\omega'_j, \omega''_j)$;
3. *harmonized* if they are both measurement and contrast harmonized.

A meta-study is *harmonized* when all constituent studies are harmonized.

Eliminating how empirical targets, and hence observed effects, vary in the design of constituent studies allows isolation of how a mechanism's effect varies from setting to setting. Harmonization is about efforts that serve to eliminate the differences between empirical findings that are due to research design, without the invocation of stronger assumptions or elaborate models. Ultimately, harmonization is a theoretical concern, and can be difficult to achieve in some

---

[5] This formulation straightforwardly generalizes to studies that focus on multiple outcomes.

applications. We discuss some practical implications of harmonization in more detail next.

2.5 Relation to the Potential Outcomes Model

Our theory of measurement, which centers on empirical targets, is intentionally abstract in order to be general enough to accommodate many concepts of research design. Many scholars – including those currently at the forefront of applied evidence accumulation efforts – view causal research designs through the potential outcomes model (or framework). Indeed, proponents of the credibility revolution advocate using the potential outcomes model to define the causal effects that serve as a measure of a mechanism's influence (e.g., Angrist & Pischke, 2008; Imbens & Wooldridge, 2009; Samii, 2016).

We now provide more general presentation of the potential outcomes model that makes explicit the role of measurement, where these considerations are typically implicit. The potential outcomes model has four ingredients. First, there is a *population of units*, indexed by $u \in \mathcal{U}$, which defines the set of units or participants that a study applies to, and broadly speaking is part of the study's setting. Sampling concerns typically revolve around how well the participants in a study represent the population of interest. Second is an intervention, which is captured by a set of *instruments*, Ω, reflected by contrasts above, that is, a contrast is a pair of instrument values (Bueno de Mesquita & Tyson, 2020). The value of the instrument, ω, can be thought of as representing the "dosage" of treatment for a subject. Third, a measurement strategy includes all the considerations that affect a researcher's choice of how to define and measure outcomes and contrasts.

Finally, the fourth ingredient is potential outcomes. It is natural to focus on the unit level, by defining *potential outcomes* as a mapping $Y_u^m(\omega \mid \theta): \mathcal{U} \times M \times \Omega \times \Theta \rightarrow \mathbb{R}$. All units in the population have a potential outcome corresponding to each level (or value) of the instrument, that is, $Y_u^m(\omega \mid \theta) \in \mathbb{R}$ is a function. The typical presentation of potential outcomes treats measurement strategies, m, and setting, θ, as implicit. Table 1 summarizes the connection between the potential outcomes model and our framework.

In practice, researchers are concerned with giving a causal interpretation to measured effects at the level of individual studies, after units have been aggregated over, and a study-level object has been defined. This study-level object is given by the choice of estimand. The most frequent choice of estimand is the *average treatment effect*, which yields the empirical target:

$$\tau_m^{\gamma=ATE}(\omega', \omega'' \mid \theta) = \mathbb{E}_u[Y_u^m(\omega'' \mid \theta) - Y_u^m(\omega' \mid \theta)], \qquad (2)$$

Table 1 Mapping between our framework and the potential outcomes model

Our Framework	Potential Outcomes Model
1 Setting, θ	Population of units, indexed by $u \in \{1, \ldots, N\}$
2 Contrast, (ω', ω'')	Intervention, captured by instruments Ω
3 Measurement strategy, m	[Implicit]
4 Incorporates setting, contrast, and measurement strategy	Potential outcome, $Y_u^m(\omega \mid \theta)$

and depends on the measurement strategy, m, contrast, (ω', ω''), and how one aggregates over units (averaging). These choices are precisely those implied by our broader concept of measurement. Of course, one could have some other aggregation rule over u (i.e., the quantile function) which would capture different kinds of (aggregate) treatment effects by changing from averaging to something else, or changing the sample by conditioning on some pre-treatment characteristics of units.

By making research design explicit in the potential outcomes model, we capture two important features that become directly relevant for evidence accumulation. First, different studies may not measure the effects of the same substantive mechanism in the same way. This has important implications for the relationship between empirical results. Although such differences have nothing to do with the mechanism of interest, they may nevertheless produce treatment effects that are different from study to study. Encoding differences in research design formally allows us to distinguish differences in how mechanisms manifest in different places from differences that are *artifacts of how the mechanism's effect was measured*. This latter feature is typically ignored in traditional presentations of the potential outcomes model, and is why our generalization is more appropriate for evidence accumulation.

Second, our formulation of potential outcomes highlights the role of various aspects of research design, and implies that a mechanism's effect necessarily depends on *how it is measured*. Specifically, there is no value of $Y_u^m(\omega \mid \theta)$ without specification of a measurement strategy, m, or a value of the instrument, ω. Consequently, our presentation of the potential outcomes model – of which standard formulations constitute a special case – reveals that a mechanism's influence results from more than some latent effect. A causal effect is the result of how a manipulation activates a causal mechanism, as well as how the influence of that mechanism is assessed quantitatively.

2.6 Application: Political Selection

We illustrate the concepts in this Element using a running example of voter information and political selection. An important aspect of democracy is that voters choose their political representatives. Voters' ability to select good (instead of bad) representatives for office depends on how much they know about their politicians, and whether voters who are informed use information about candidate quality when they have it. To address the link between voter information and political selection, a large number of field experiments seek to empirically evaluate the extent to which voters are responsive to information about candidates. The research network Evidence in Governance and Politics (EGAP) conducted its first multisite coordinated randomized controlled trial – known as a Metaketa – on this very topic. In so doing, EGAP funded the commission of seven experiments that provided voters with information about incumbents and/or challengers to see if the provision of information changes vote choice (Dunning et al., 2019a; Dunning et al., 2019b).

The Metaketa experiments that we discuss have a number of common features to which we will make reference. A treatment group is assigned to receive information about an incumbent politician or a candidate. Outcomes from the treatment group are compared to those from a status-quo control group, which consists of voters who have not been given additional information by experimenters. We discuss this class of experiments for two reasons. First, there are well-established theories of political selection that detail how the provision of good or bad news about a politician or candidate should affect vote choice (e.g., Ashworth, 2012; Ashworth et al., 2018; Besley, 2006; Ferejohn, 1986). Consequently, we can draw on common theories and models to articulate mechanisms of political selection.[6]

Suppose that there are two politicians, an incumbent and a challenger, competing in an election decided by a simple majority. Each politician has a private type, $t \in \{0, 1\}$, where $t = 0$ indicates a "bad" type and $t = 1$ indicates a "good" type. The probability that a politician is a good type is given by $P(t = 1) = q \in (0, 1)$. Many empirical studies of information and accountability explicitly or implicitly stratify on the quality of the informational signal about the incumbent.[7] As such, they study the effect of a good signal (e.g., that the incumbent is "not corrupt") in districts where the signal is good separately from districts where the signal is bad (e.g., that the incumbent is "corrupt").

---

[6] For other theoretical treatments of information and accountability experiments, see Izzo et al. (2022) and Slough (2024).

[7] When voter prior beliefs about the incumbent are measured ex-ante, some studies like those in (Dunning et al., 2019a) stratify on the voter's prior relative to the informational signal.

For brevity, we focus on the case where the signal is good since the analysis otherwise is similar.

A district has a unit mass of voters whose preferences for the incumbent are given by a district-level bias, G, and an idiosyncratic individual preference, v_i, with support $[-1, 1]$, that is distributed across voters according to some mean-zero distribution function F. Voter i's payoff from the incumbent is

$$v_i + G + t_I,$$

where t_I is the incumbent's type. A voter's payoff from the challenger is normalized to t_C. One can think of $G + v_i$ as voter i's ideological preference for/against the incumbent relative to the challenger. Voting is costless and we assume that (1) when indifferent, a voter votes for the incumbent; and (2) voters do not choose weakly dominated strategies.

A politician's type is not known and some voters commonly see a signal of incumbent type, $x \in \{0, 1\}$, where

$$P(x = 1 \mid t_I = 1) = P(x = 0 \mid t_I = 0) = p \in [1/2, 1].$$

The proportion of voters receiving the signal, x, is $\mu \in [0, 1]$, while the remaining proportion of voters receive no signal. Whether a single voter receives a signal is independent of whether other voters receive a signal. No signals are received about the challenger's type, t_C.

A voter who sees signal x prefers the incumbent when

$$v_i + G + P(t_I = 1 \mid x) \geq P(t_C = 1).$$

Since the posterior belief, given the signal, is

$$P(t = 1 \mid x = 1) = \frac{pq}{pq + (1 - p)(1 - q)},$$

voter i votes for the incumbent following a good signal ($x = 1$) whenever

$$v_i + G + \frac{pq}{pq + (1 - p)(1 - q)} \geq q,$$

which simplifies to

$$v_i \geq \frac{q(1 - q)(1 - 2p)}{pq + (1 - p)(1 - q)} - G.$$

The mechanism in this model is called adverse selection, and it represents voters' inability to perfectly select politicians since bad incumbents sometimes benefit from good signals and good incumbents sometimes get bad signals. The mechanism's effect manifests through the term:

$$\frac{q(1 - q)(1 - 2p)}{pq + (1 - p)(1 - q)}. \tag{3}$$

This expression reflects the population's change in belief (from the prior) about the incumbent's type as a result of the good signal, $x = 1$, all else equal. If the mechanism were not active (as in the case of an uninformative signal, that is, $p = \frac{1}{2}$), expression (3) would be equal to 0. We treat the case in which the voter observes no signal as observationally equivalent to this uninformative signal.

Notice that the adverse selection mechanism cannot be directly observed, but there are several possible measures of the mechanism's effect. We first consider the outcome measurement strategy that focuses on the incumbent's vote share in the model, following a good signal. Since μ voters receive the good signal, vote share is given by

$$V(\mu; G) = \mu \left(1 - F \left(\frac{q(1 - q)(1 - 2p)}{pq + (1 - p)(1 - q)} - G \right) \right) + (1 - \mu)(1 - F(-G)).$$

Another measurement strategy, used to detect the effect of the adverse selection mechanism, uses the reelection rule, also following a good signal, which under simple majority voting is

$$R(\mu; G) = \begin{cases} 1 & \text{if } V(\mu; G) \geq \frac{1}{2} \\ 0 & \text{otherwise.} \end{cases}$$

This says that the incumbent is reelected whenever $R(\mu; G) = 1$.

An information experiment aims to augment the share of the electorate that observes the signal. In other words, in a status quo, suppose that share μ' of the electorate observes the signal. The experiment then increases this share to $\mu'' > \mu'$. It is important to note that many experiments do not explicitly measure μ' or μ'' (and it is likely impractical to do so in many settings). However, experimentalists often talk about "stronger" versus "weaker" treatments. As will become clear when we assess empirical targets, the effect of a mechanism on a single outcome measure will depend on the strength of treatment, μ'', relative to the status-quo information environment, μ'.

Given our outcome measures – vote share and reelection rate – as well as the contrast of interest, μ' and μ'', we can specify empirical targets after an estimand is selected. The estimand used most frequently by experimentalists is the average treatment effect, which aggregates over districts in our model. Suppose that districts vary according to G, that is, G is distributed across districts according to some distribution. Then, average vote share across districts is

$$\mathbb{E}_G[V(\mu; G)],$$

and the reelection rate among districts is

$$\mathbb{E}_G[1_{\{R(\mu;G)=1\}}] = P(R(\mu; G) = 1) = P(V(\mu; G) \geq \tfrac{1}{2}).$$

By the Liebniz integral rule, the empirical targets are as follows. For vote share the empirical target is

$$\tau_V^{ATE}(\mu', \mu'' \mid \theta) = (\mu'' - \mu')\mathbb{E}_G\left[\frac{dV(\mu; G)}{d\mu}\right],$$

whereas for reelection the empirical target is

$$\tau_R^{ATE}(\mu', \mu'' \mid \theta) = (\mu'' - \mu')\frac{dP(V(\mu; G) \geq \tfrac{1}{2})}{d\mu}$$

$$= (\mu'' - \mu')\frac{dP(V(\mu; G) \geq \tfrac{1}{2})}{dV(\mu; G)} \cdot \mathbb{E}_G\left[\frac{dV(\mu; G)}{d\mu}\right].$$

Both expressions quantify the effect of the adverse selection mechanism, but they do so in different ways. The empirical targets provided by vote share and reelection rate, respectively, are, in general, not equivalent to each other. In particular, only when

$$\frac{dP(V(\mu; G) \geq \tfrac{1}{2})}{dV(\mu; G)} = 1$$

do the different measures of adverse selection yield the same empirical target. This implies that (in the model) the empirical targets are equivalent if and only if $V(\mu; G)$ is uniformly distributed. To guarantee this requires a specific distribution of G across districts, which, although straightforward to derive, reflects aspects of the external world that are generally outside researcher control.

Furthermore, by inspection, we can see that for either outcome, vote share or re-election, the measured effect also depends on the contrast that is utilized, represented in the model by $\mu'' - \mu'$. The difference between the empirical targets reflects our point that there is no "true effect" of the adverse selection mechanism. Instead, the measured effect of adverse selection, even in a world as simple as that in our model, depends on how that effect is elicited and measured. Thus, the choices a researcher makes, in terms of measurement strategies and contrasts, affect what the researcher ultimately sees.

3 External Validity

Scholars typically seek to make inferences and develop explanations about broad substantive phenomena, meaning those that are not tied to any specific context, sample, or population. This kind of generality is a necessary ingredient of satisfying substantive explanations, since "it seems altogether reasonable to maintain that any adequate explanation of a particular fact must be, in principle, generalizable into an explanation of a suitable sort of regularity" (Salmon, 1984, p. 276). External validity reflects a concern with the relationship between this kind of general regularity and research design, and refers to a cluster of distinct concepts that relate empirical targets across multiple settings.

To illustrate the kinds of issues that arise when thinking about external validity, consider an example. Suppose that we are interested in the effect of an undergraduate student advising program on student grades. To measure this effect, we select a simple random sample of 300 undergraduates at New York University (NYU), of whom we randomly assign approximately 150 to control and 150 to the new advising program (treatment). The results of our study tell us something about the population of NYU undergraduates. Up to this point, nothing about external validity has been invoked, just sampling, estimation, and inference. In other words, external validity is *not* about transporting a treatment effect from a random sample to the population from which the sample is drawn. Instead, it is about transporting evidence outside of that population.

The estimated treatment effects that might be obtained from our hypothetical study using NYU undergraduates tells us nothing about, for instance, University of Rochester undergraduates. One needs to know, at least, that the mechanism activated by the advising program on NYU undergraduates has broader application than just undergraduates at NYU, and would also activate on undergraduates at other universities given the same advising program. Suppose that we also conducted our study on University of Rochester undergraduates and found a similar effect to that from NYU. This suggests that the mechanism may be at play in both locations, but ultimately provides no empirical information about the program's effects on undergraduates at Columbia University (for example). Any belief that the program would have a similar effect on undergraduates at Columbia, given empirical information on NYU and Rochester undergraduates, reflects a theoretical commitment about how broadly the mechanism under study applies. The expectation that finding a similar result in two places – instead of just one – constitutes evidence of something more general reflects an ontological and metaphysical commitment that a common mechanism exists, and manifests broadly enough to be present outside of the settings in which it has been initially observed.

When can we learn about, or assess, the external validity of a finding by accumulating evidence? In order to understand how external validity relates to evidence accumulation efforts, we need precise definitions of external validity: what it is, when it is present, and how to know when it holds. External validity is best understood as a cluster of concepts, which are united by their efforts to relate empirical findings from multiple settings. Different concepts assume different relationships, typically by imposing more or less structure on the relationship between studies, which we refer to as the **cross-study environment**. This purported structure encodes metaphysical commitments about this environment.

External validity characterizes how empirical targets change when settings change. These concepts tell us what information an inference in one setting provides about other settings where a mechanism has not necessarily been measured. This means that external validity cannot be faithfully characterized as an entirely empirical concept. It always reflects some theoretical commitments. Since empirical targets are defined within a study, and external validity centers on the set of relationships between empirical targets across sites, a theoretical formulation of external validity must engage with empirical targets. In this section, we focus on two distinct ways scholars formulate external validity theoretically: **projectivism** and **cross-sectionalism**.

3.1 Projectivism

The first, and arguably most common, formulation of external validity is **projectivism**, which conceptualizes external validity as being when a theoretical effect *projects from a source onto a destination*.

PROJECTIVIST EXTERNAL VALIDITY

An empirical target has projective external validity if there is a **source**, Δ, a set of **destinations**, $\{\delta_i\}$, and a mapping, π, such that for every δ_i,

$$\pi(\Delta, i) = \delta_i.$$

Projectivist formulations of external validity differ depending on the source under consideration, Δ, the set of destinations, $\{\delta_i\}$, and the projection used, π. In particular, some projections are vertical, where the source, Δ, is a theoretical object and a single empirical finding that has been observed, δ_i, is thought to be a projection from that source. Other projective formulations are horizontal, where the source is an actual empirical finding, which projects onto other potential empirical findings, $\{\delta_i\}$. In this case, the source, Δ, is an effect that has been observed and measured, and the set of destinations comprises a set of empirical findings that may (or may not) have been observed.

Projective formulations of external validity also rely on an underlying model of the cross-study environment that details, to varying degrees of specification, the structural relationship between the source, Δ, and the set of destinations, $\{\delta_i\}$. In practice, much needs to be known (or assumed) about the cross-study environment in order to define empirical targets, turn cross-study features into estimation targets, and then subsequently interpret the resulting estimates.

3.1.1 Grand Sampling

One of the most common formulations of external validity uses sampling as a metaphor, and posits a hierarchical model of the cross-study environment. Similar to how one conceptualizes a sample from a single study as being drawn from some population of interest, Findley et al. (2021, p. 368) argue that "[e]xternal validity captures the extent to which inferences drawn from a given study's sample apply to a broader population or other target populations." What ties together such vertical projective formulations of external validity is imagining a **grand population** of individuals, subjects, or units that exist, have ever existed, or could ever exist. An individual study, then, conducted in country X in year T is simply a sample from this grand population.

Various constraints having to do with geographic or temporal dependence mean that the grand population cannot be studied or sampled from in a straightforward manner, thus dividing the grand population into subpopulations, such as individuals existing on Earth in the twenty-first century (Munger, 2023). The grand population, to which a single study speaks, is defined as the set of all places, times, and so on where the underlying mechanism in a single study manifests. A grand population-level estimate, then, can be estimated using a single study through statistical techniques applied to the observed sample (Gerber & Green, 2012, Chapter 11).

What makes the grand sampling approach projective is the relationship between the source, often called the population average treatment effect (PATE), and the destination, typically referred to as the sample average treatment effect (SATE) from sample i. In this formulation, the relationship

$$\pi(PATE, i) = SATE_i = PATE + b_i + \varepsilon_i \qquad (4)$$

is a typical example of the vertical projective formulation, where b_i is some form of "site selection bias" (Allcott, 2015), or "external validity bias" (Andrews & Oster, 2019; Egami & Hartman 2023; Findley et al., 2021), and ε_i represents some kind of error term. When focused on inferring the source – typically the PATE – the terms b_i and ε_i are not of substantive interest, since a single study's finding is thought to be a projection from what one would obtain if one were able to study the grand population directly. In particular, when considering the effect of a treatment on an outcome, the goal is to use the estimate of the effect from a single destination to learn about the effect of that treatment *if it were applied to the source.*

A key strength of the grand sampling approach is that it substantially reduces the complexity of any theoretical or conceptual issues surrounding the accumulation of empirical evidence. It does so by treating such issues as though they are simply *estimation problems*, rather than reflecting fundamental substantive mismatches between different studies. Since it is considerably easier to deal with comparability problems when a single study measures the grand population parameter with noise, rather than quantities that may be systematically unrelated across studies, the grand population approach has great flexibility when it comes to producing estimands for a given collection of data. Various estimators have been developed to move from sample estimands to grand population parameters (i.e., Cole & Stuart, 2010; Gechter & Meager, 2021; Kern et al., 2016).

By converting all features of the cross-study environment, and any potential problems that might arise, to estimation challenges, grand sampling approaches treat data collected from the cross-study environment in a very specific way. Namely, they exclusively leverage heterogeneity between individuals in the sample as the source of potential heterogeneity in treatment effects. While this form of heterogeneity is important, it is not the only form of heterogeneity that may be present. Specifically, grand sampling approaches presume away across-study heterogeneity that may be due to differences in research design or failures of "external validity." Our theoretical framework provides concepts and results focused on these less discussed forms of heterogeneity.

In some cases, the grand sampling approach may be very natural, for instance, when taking a sample of cancer patients at Strong Memorial Hospital at the University of Rochester as relating to the population of individuals who potentially have (or have been diagnosed with) cancer. In this example, the grand population is very clear, and although it cannot be studied directly, this does not undermine the quantitative relationship between the study participants and individuals who were not part of the sample. In other contexts, however, the grand sampling approach is less natural – yet nevertheless applied. For the purposes of illustration, we take a somewhat extreme example. Many studies are devoted to measuring the impact of economic shocks on conflict. Does it make sense to think of the external validity of, say, an opportunity cost mechanism, in the way projective formulations do? In particular, is a single instance of an economic shock, and its relation to conflict, projected from some source occurrence? Are actual economic shocks, taken to be projected from a grand population of all potential economic shocks, including those that never, or are yet to, occur? Are properties of this set an object of substantive interest? In this extreme example, the grand sampling approach strains credulity because it relies on the existence of an object – a grand population of all potential economic shocks – that is an artifact of the measurement model.

3.1.2 Imputation and Prediction

In vertical projective views of external validity, the source, such as a population average treatment effect, is a theoretical object, and may never be observed directly. A different projective formulation of external validity is horizontal, where the source, Δ, is itself an actual empirical finding, and the set of destinations can include other empirical findings or even hypothetical empirical findings.

The most well-known application of a horizontal projective approach to external validity is *transportability* (Pearl & Bareinboim, 2011, 2014). This view approaches the projection of a study's finding from one place to another using imputation. In particular, taking an original study's finding from one setting, the source Δ, and projecting it onto the destination δ_i. The imputed effect is interpreted as if the same study were conducted in the destination setting, i, rather than only the source setting, Δ. The imputation at the heart of this approach is accomplished using a "transport formula" which takes observables that have been collected in both the source and destination settings, such as observational demographic data, and uses differences in those observables to create a reweighted average.

A closely related approach, which is also consistent with a horizontal projectivist view of external validity, is Egami and Hartman (2023), who develop the "contextual exclusion restriction" which holds that unit-level treatment effects do not change with unobserved contextual factors. Consequently, by controlling for observed contextual differences, a researcher is assured that there is no difference in potential outcomes across settings. It is worth noting that transportability and the related contextual exclusion restriction differ from grand sampling because the source is an actual empirical finding, wherever, whenever, and however it was produced. The set of destinations include any places where the study *could* have been conducted, which are now informed, via the transport formula or contextual exclusion restriction, by the original study.

Another example of a horizontal projectivist approach is Fariss and Jones (2018) and differs substantially from transportability and the contextual exclusion restriction. In particular, Fariss and Jones (2018) suggest using the predictive success of an actual empirical finding on other empirical findings to judge whether the mechanism of interest has external validity.

Starting with the source finding, Δ, Fariss and Jones (2018) suggest using $N \geq 1$ destination findings, $\{\delta_i\}_{i=1}^{N}$, to compute

$$-\left(\Delta - N^{-1} \sum_{i=1}^{N} \delta_i\right)^2, \tag{5}$$

which uses mean-square error to measure the predictive accuracy of the source finding, Δ, for findings collected in a number of destinations, $\{\delta_i\}$. Fariss and Jones (2018) suggest a number of practical ways to implement (5), using penalty functions that are more robust (albeit more elaborate) and assessing predictive scope, but which are beyond the scope of this Element.

What differs between the predictive approach of Fariss and Jones (2018) and the imputation approaches of Pearl and Bareinboim (2011, 2014) and Egami and Hartman (2023) is how they relate to external validity. Specifically, the former is evaluative, whereas the latter is speculative. Specifically, Fariss and Jones (2018) advocate for approaches to evidence accumulation that use predictive accuracy (however defined) as a way of evaluating or judging the external validity of a particular empirical finding. High predictive accuracy, according to Fariss and Jones, provides evidence that a mechanism has external validity. By contrast, transportability and the contextual exclusion restriction are speculative because they endorse imputation of effects without actually conducting studies in new settings, relying instead on confidence in the method for imputation and a presupposition of some form of external validity; we revisit this in Chapter 7.

3.2 Cross-sectionalism

A **cross-sectional** formulation of external validity treats individual studies as separate and distinct entities that may be related, but in ways that can be unknown or underspecified. Similar to the way that the grand sampling formulation uses sampling as a metaphor for the cross-study environment, cross-sectionalism uses the most common data structure – a cross-section – as a metaphor for the cross-study environment. What makes cross-sectionalism different from projectivism is that thinking of external validity as a property of a cross-section of studies does not require some abstract source, such as the population average treatment effect, or an elaborate structural model linking the source to all destination findings across various studies, such as a latent variable model. Moreover, cross-sectionalist formulations of external validity do not assume the existence of a theoretical grand population from which individual studies are "drawn." Instead, each study essentially comprises a unique data point, where the data points associated with different studies are symmetrically connected through the presence of a mechanism. Thus, cross-sectionalism is a more general formulation of external validity, that is, it is consistent with an elaborate structure of the cross-study environment common to projective formulations, but does not require such elaborate quantitative structures to make sense of the results obtained from meta-studies.

There are several different formulations of the relationship between constituent studies, each of which is consistent with a cross-sectional formulation of external validity, and we focus on two. The way that these different formulations differ is in how they relate empirical targets in different settings. The most natural formulation, originally articulated in Slough and Tyson (2023, Definition 7) applied to meta-analysis (see Chapter 5), is that empirical targets need to be the same across settings. Recall that empirical targets are represented by the treatment effect function, $\tau_m^\gamma(\omega', \omega'' \mid \theta)$, for a given measurement strategy, m, contrast, (ω', ω''), and setting, θ, evaluated with an estimand γ.

EXACT EXTERNAL VALIDITY

A mechanism has **exact external validity** from setting θ to θ' if for almost every measurement strategy $m \in M$, and almost every contrast (ω', ω''), when evaluated with estimand γ:

$$\tau_m^\gamma(\omega', \omega'' \mid \theta) = \tau_m^\gamma(\omega', \omega'' \mid \theta').$$

A mechanism is externally valid if it has external validity for almost all contrasts and almost all measurement strategies.

Exact external validity characterizes the relationship between empirical targets as they appear in different settings, that is, across θ. A key strength of the cross-sectional formulation of external validity is that the precise notion of external validity can be tailored to the application at hand.

Consider another example, which draws on Slough and Tyson (2024)'s examination of replication. A researcher may not be interested in whether the empirical targets across settings are the same, but instead, on evaluating whether the *sign* of the empirical targets are the same across settings.

SIGN-CONGRUENT EXTERNAL VALIDITY

A mechanism has **sign-congruent external validity** from setting θ to θ' if for almost every measurement strategy $m \in M$, and almost every contrast (ω', ω''), when evaluated with estimand γ:

$$sign\{\tau_m^\gamma(\omega', \omega'' \mid \theta)\} = sign\{\tau_m^\gamma(\omega', \omega'' \mid \theta')\}.$$

A mechanism is sign-congruent externally valid if it has sign-congruent external validity for almost all contrasts and almost all measurement strategies.

This illustrates how the precise formulation of external validity depends on the substantive question being addressed. In particular, by choosing the exact relationship between empirical targets, one chooses how they expect empirical targets to be related across settings. Cross-sectional formulations of external validity provide greater flexibility in thinking about the relationship between empirical targets. In particular, other cross-sectional formulations of external validity follow by changing the relationship between empirical targets, that is, by using a function other than the identity function (exact external validity) or the sign function (sign-congruent external validity).

In the second part (Applications), we show how different approaches to evidence accumulation, for example, meta-analysis, replication, or extrapolation exercises, have different relationships to external validity. For example, in its most agnostic form, meta-analysis combines empirical findings across studies (however one formulates external validity), and is consistent with a cross-sectionalist formulation of external validity.

Cross-sectionalism, as opposed to some versions of projectivism, is not a matter of taste or style, but instead constitutes an important set of theoretical and philosophical commitments about the cross-study environment. Under projectivism, noting that the source, Δ, and each destination, δ_i, can be thought of as empirical targets, the projective mapping, π, details a specific relationship between empirical targets. For instance, denoting the source setting as θ_0, the source can be formulated as

$$\Delta \equiv \tau_m^\gamma(\omega', \omega'' | \theta_0),$$

which depends (at least implicitly) on aspects of the research design in the source setting. This is a key insight of measurement perspectivism, namely, without a natural "true" research design, even the source will produce a different effect depending on the research design used to articulate the source effect. Since the mapping, π, reflects the quantitative relationship between the source target and the destination target(s), we have the relationship

$$\pi(\tau_{m_0}^{\gamma_i}(\omega_0', \omega_0'' | \theta_0), i) = \tau_{m_i}^{\gamma_i}(\omega_i', \omega_i'' | \theta_i) = \delta_i,$$

for every i. Absent an explicit formulation of the research design used to express the source, the projective mapping, π, thus becomes implicitly linked to some research design, and this implicit design grounds inference about the source made from analysis of any set of destinations. Findings from a single study correspond to a single empirical target; they do not simply project to other empirical targets without a theory of how they do so. This highlights that researchers need to consider what ties constituent studies together and what theoretical commitments a particular approach to evidence accumulation entails.

3.3 A Trade-off between Internal and External Validity?

Different formulations of external validity speak to similar underlying concerns: What produces common substantive phenomena in different places and at different times? How can we assess whether a mechanism has a similar influence in different settings? In this section, we have highlighted two of the most common ways scholars think about external validity: projectivism and cross-sectionalism. Before moving on, it is worth stressing that defining external validity in terms of empirical targets clarifies what kind of relationship (if any) arises between internal and external validity.

That a single study's internal validity is somehow related to its external validity, either by enhancing it or detracting from it, rests on a core confusion. Specifically, it is *impossible to know* whether a similar effect would obtain in different contexts or samples, taking only information at the level of a single study, regardless of the quality of that study. Put differently, asking whether a finding from a study has external validity, based solely on the properties of that single study, is a category error. One cannot assess external validity empirically without accumulating evidence from multiple places, times, and contexts, and comparing that evidence.

There is no trade-off between internal and external validity.[8] Instead, internal validity is a necessary condition for external validity because it is about the fidelity of the connection between a mechanism and its measured effect, that is, the empirical target the mechanism produces. Without internal validity, the influence of a mechanism has not been measured, and as a result it cannot be credibly compared or combined with estimates from another study, even if the mechanism is indeed present in both studies.

3.3.1 Parallelism and the Latour Critique

Many conceptions of the trade-off between internal and external validity revolve around the "artificiality" induced by the stringent conditions needed for internal validity with design-based approaches. The concern has been prominent in experimental economics due to the observation that laboratory experiments differ from field experiments because researchers have more control over laboratory than field conditions, in particular, over subjects' preferences. **Parallelism** refers to the extent to which empirical findings that have been measured in an artificial setting (like a laboratory) extend to natural settings like a field experiment (Guala, 2005; Smith, 1982).

---

[8] Gailmard (2021, p. 96) makes a similar point: "external validity cannot exist without internal validity."

Parallelism, and its relationship to external validity, largely emerged as a response to prominent concerns about studies that draw so heavily on experiments, especially those conducted in a laboratory. The most mature (and perhaps extreme) presentations of this critique are Latour and Woolgar (1986) and Latour (1993), who argue that the setup of experimental conditions, which hold fixed mitigating factors, ultimately produce an empirical finding that says nothing about the external world. In other words, even if a research design permits credible estimation of a causal effect, such effects have no bearing on what would be experienced in the external world, and thus ultimately say nothing about the world outside of the laboratory.

Latour and Woolgar (1986) and Latour (1993) argue further that results obtained through experimentation are better understood as constructed rather than discovered, because they are obtained in such carefully manipulated circumstances. Consequently, manipulating natural phenomena in a controlled (or contrived) environment produces findings that are ineluctably non-generalizable, and are thus not parallel to the natural world. Analogous critiques have been lodged against experiments and credibility-centered research designs more generally (Deaton, 2010; Deaton & Cartwright, 2018; Huber, 2017). Ultimately, these critiques, like Latour and Woolgar (1986) and Latour (1993), conflate differences in empirical targets that emerge from differences in research design, with differences in empirical targets that emerge from changes in the setting. Without stronger assumptions about how treatment effects vary in study design and/or setting, one cannot assert a trade-off between internal or external validity.

Responses to Latour's critique and related criticisms begin from the acknowledgment that differences can emerge as artifacts of study design *or* a lack of external validity. In the context of lab experiments, Guala (2003) suggests that such critiques, and especially Latour, are too "radically localist" when interpreting the implications of experimental results. They essentially correspond to a whole-scale rejection of external validity. Instead, Guala (2005) interprets parallelism as addressing a particular type of robustness, applied to a study design *or* mechanism, which can be assessed from study to study.

Pritchett and Sandefur (2015) build upon the parallelist view to bridge the gap between experiments and observational studies in the case of microfinance. They consider how to measure the extent to which experimental findings inform observational research, and thus are linked despite differences in how they are measured (see also Meager (2019)). Both reactions implicitly stress the importance of evidence accumulation as a response to critiques of the experimentalist approach.

3.4 Application: External Validity and Political Selection

Questions of external validity ask how empirical targets, $\tau_m^\gamma(\omega', \omega'' \mid \theta)$, vary in setting, $\theta \in \Theta$. Recall that in Chapter 2, we describe an intervention that provides voters with information about an incumbent in the lead-up to an election. We will again focus on the case of good news: when the informational signal suggests that an incumbent is more likely to be a good type. To focus our discussion further, we consider only incumbent vote share, $V(\mu; G)$. Analogous considerations hold for other outcomes. We illustrate concepts of external validity through two examples.

Example #1: Different pools of candidates. Consider the possibility that the share of good types ($t = 1$) among the candidate pool may be different in different settings. In our model, this is reflected when the prior probability that politicians are a good type depends on the setting, so that $P(t = 1 \mid \theta) = q_\theta$. We can then write vote share for the incumbent in setting θ as

$$V(\mu; G \mid \theta) = \mu\left(1 - F\left(\frac{q_\theta(1 - q_\theta)(1 - 2p)}{pq_\theta + (1 - p)(1 - q_\theta)} - G\right)\right) + (1 - \mu)(1 - F(-G)).$$

Incumbent vote share is an upside down U-shaped function of q_θ, implying that the adverse selection mechanism produces different effects when there are different shares of good types in the candidate pool. In other words, q_θ is a feature of a setting, θ, that interacts with the adverse selection mechanism to produce an effect on incumbent vote share. Does such a difference between setting reflect a failure of external validity? Although the mechanism across settings is the same in our model (by construction), such a difference nevertheless reflects a failure of exact external validity.[9]

Providing more voters with a signal of incumbent quality, when the signal is good, leads to higher incumbent vote share for any value of $q \in (0, 1)$. Consequently, increasing the share of voters receiving the signal, μ, should yield a *positive* average treatment effect in all settings, regardless of the respective candidate pools. This shows that sign-congruent external validity is satisfied for incumbent vote share. Specifically, the adverse selection mechanism should produce a positively signed effect on incumbent vote share even when different settings have different candidate pools. This illustrates why the concept of sign-congruent external validity can be useful in a variety of applications.

---

[9] An outcome measure of the mechanism that does not involve the pool of candidate quality would not have this problem and thus might exhibit exact external validity.

Now, consider how this example fits with the grand sampling (projectivist) approach to external validity. Researchers conduct an information experiment in setting i where the share of good types in the candidate pool is q_{θ_i}. They seek to learn about the effect of good news in a source setting, θ_0, where the share of good types among candidates is ostensibly q_{θ_0}. Describing the substantive relevance of the source remains a challenge because defining this grand population is not straightforward. Is the grand population composed of all candidates currently running for office? Or all potential candidates who could have (or may) ever run for office? Since incumbent vote share, $V(\mu; G \mid \theta)$, is U-shaped, is the grand population pool on the same part of the curve (upward or downward sloping) as the setting i? Without a clear definition of the source population, or the mapping that determines how the source gives rise to the destinations under study, inferences about the source depend on unspecified assumptions of the research design underlying the source's definition.

Example #2: Different status quo levels of information. Consider an environment in which different shares of the electorate observe the informational signal in the absence of the intervention. All other characteristics of the environments are identical, including the prior probability that politicians are good, q. The idea here is that some settings feature more informed voters than others in the absence of an intervention. To denote this formally, we will say that μ_θ can vary in setting, θ. Importantly, this means that the "control" value of the contrast may vary across settings. This is a common feature of coordinated experiments that use the status quo as a control group.

Recall that external validity is about the relationship between a mechanism's influence, and how that influence is quantified and measured. Focusing again on the vote share for the incumbent, $V(\mu; G)$, it is straightforward to see that the average treatment effect of good news has exact external validity between settings θ and θ' if and only if

$$(\mu_\theta'' - \mu_\theta')\mathbb{E}_G\left[\frac{dV(\mu; G)}{d\mu}\right] = (\mu_{\theta'}'' - \mu_{\theta'}')\mathbb{E}_G\left[\frac{dV(\mu; G)}{d\mu}\right].$$

For this expression to hold, researchers would need to carefully choose the saturation of the information treatments μ_θ'' and $\mu_{\theta'}''$ to elicit the same change in the level of information. Ultimately this is a design choice: Researchers could, in principle, strengthen or weaken a treatment by providing information to more or less of the electorate. The expression above illustrates the importance of harmonization in achieving external validity, since it depends only on the difference $\mu_\theta'' - \mu_\theta'$, showing that one can harmonize a contrast without perfectly harmonizing both instruments. Harmonization is thus not about ensuring that all treatments are literally the same, but that they serve the same role in the expression of empirical targets. At the same time, it is clear that harmonization is difficult to achieve with status quo controls. In the context of this example, one would need to know the share of voters in the status quo who observe the signal in order to select the treatment instrument to harmonize the contrast.

In this example, increasing the share of the electorate that observes good news about the incumbent should always increase incumbent vote share even if harmonization is not achievable in practice. This should yield positive average treatment effects of good news on incumbent vote share. But the reason that we observe different (if similarly signed) estimates is because the design is not harmonized. These considerations of different designs in different settings are distinct from concerns about external validity, which are about how the effect of the mechanism varies in different settings under the same design. While the empirical targets should maintain the same positive sign in this example, readers should not equate an externally valid mechanism, measured under a non-harmonized design, to a mechanism that only exhibits sign-congruent external validity but is measured using a harmonized design (as in Example #1).

Projective concepts of external validity formalize or parameterize differences in the effect of a mechanism across settings. These concepts are not naturally equipped to handle situations like this second example in which different research designs (here, distinct contrasts) induce differences in the effect of a mechanism. While one may be interested in assessing the robustness of an intervention technology to stronger or weaker versions of treatment, for example, these considerations are distinct from questions about the mechanism's influence in different settings.

4 Uniting Principles

Evidence accumulation can take a variety of different forms, including, but not limited to, replication and meta-analysis. The primary question that researchers and consumers need to ask when evaluating the results from a study that unites evidence from multiple studies is whether there are reasons to presume that some feature of the external world (e.g., a mechanism) is present (or active) across studies. Moreover, one cannot neglect consideration of how different studies are tied together *quantitatively*, meaning how their empirical targets relate to each other in a quantitative sense.

To justify any approach to evidence accumulation across study settings, there must be something that unites the constituent studies that make up a meta-study. The most prominent view is that constituent studies can be united by a *common mechanism*, which underlies the empirical findings that have been collected across different settings. In such cases, evidence accumulation is about studying *that* mechanism, abstracting from other details that might be present within a single setting but which are not essential to the mechanism. The existence of broadly applicable mechanisms – that transcend space, time, or setting – is a critical feature of empirical science. This premise rests on the existence of discoverable phenomena that extend beyond the idiosyncratic circumstances in which a single instance of a given phenomenon is observed.

To illustrate, consider two experiments on participation in collective action where group size is manipulated. In one, an experimentalist increases group size (relative to some control size) and in another the experimentalist decreases group size (relative to some other control size). In each case, the intervention should influence collective action through the same mechanism: incentives to free ride. However, even if both interventions tap into the same phenomenon, there is no reason that they should do so in exactly the same way. In particular, there is no guarantee that the two studies share a *quantitative* relationship. As a result, the two studies of collective action should not produce the same treatment effect. If they did, it would be by accident, for example, because differences in measurement strategies perfectly offset the difference in treatments. So, how can studies that tap into the same phenomenon nevertheless be brought together quantitatively?

This example shows how a large part of the process of evidence accumulation relies on a theoretical understanding of the cross-study environment, addressing what holds together all the constituent studies quantitatively. In this section, we develop the idea of **uniting principles**, which are the set of theoretical arguments and assumptions that bring together different studies under consideration in a meta-study. Uniting principles are important because evidence accumulation relies – implicitly or explicitly – on imparting a meta-study's findings with things like a descriptive or causal interpretation.[10]

Empirical targets express how a mechanism and a research design combine to produce a measured quantitative effect. Consequently, empirical targets serve as the quantitative objects that need to be united across different constituent studies of the same mechanism. For this reason, they comprise the key theoretical object that underlies evidence accumulation. Having a quantitative object relating different studies is important because "what is desirable [about quantitative knowledge] is the strength and *severity of the argument*

---

[10] Meta-studies can also answer some methodological or meta-scientific questions by combining evidence from (conceptually) unrelated studies. For example, scholars have examined evidence of publication bias by examining the distribution of T-statistics across unrelated published studies (Brodeur et al., 2020; Gerber & Malhotra, 2008). We view this descriptive use of meta-studies as distinct from efforts to accumulate evidence about common mechanisms.

that is afforded by a special kind of experimental knowledge" (Mayo, 1996, p. 44). In particular, quantitative knowledge facilitates the kind of reliability of manipulation that promotes the accumulation of scientific knowledge (Hacking, 1983).

The perspectivist argument developed in Chapter 2 shows how casual arguments that justify pulling together different studies are not enough. Specifically, even though a mechanism may, without question, be present in every constituent study, if the quantitative relationship between empirical targets across studies is not specified, then the results obtained from a meta-study are *not quantitative*. Consequently, evidence accumulation necessarily requires a detailing of how empirical targets across studies are related at the theoretical level. This implies that the relationship between empirical targets ultimately rests on a substantive argument and cannot be established statistically.

Any accumulation of quantitative evidence that combines, compares, or extrapolates empirical findings necessarily invokes a set of uniting principles, which determine what is assumed and what can be learned about the generality of phenomena. When the goal is to learn about a common mechanism by examining its influence in different settings, these settings must be united by a common articulation of that mechanism that specifies quantitative relationships. Ideally, there would exist a theoretical model that represents each setting as a particular "instantiation" of the same underlying model (Orzack & Sober, 1993), thus making the uniting principles explicit and naturally comparable.

4.1 The Importance of Uniting Principles

To illustrate the importance of qualitative and quantitative alignment of empirical targets through uniting principles we continue our analysis of the political selection model introduced in Chapter 2. In Chapters 2 and 3, we considered an information treatment that serves as a signal about an incumbent's type (good or bad). If a voter sees the signal, then they update their belief about the incumbent's type before casting their ballot. In this section, we consider this same experiment as well as a different type of information experiment in order to make concrete the importance of uniting principles. Comparing these two kinds of experiments elucidates the key considerations needed to ensure that the effect of information treatments are quantitatively comparable across different settings.

4.1.1 An Alternative Mechanism: Voter Preferences

Our running example has focused on the manipulation that provides information about an incumbent politician's type (good or bad) to voters. In particular, the content of the information provided to voters is about some feature of the politician that is relevant for future performance, that is, whether the politician is corrupt or not. Suppose, instead, that the content of the signal is about some feature that changes the preferences of voters. For instance, a political scandal that revealed that the incumbent is "icky" or some unexpected aspect of the incumbent's background makes them more desirable to voters, like a celebrity endorsement.

A shock to the incumbent's popularity works differently than information about some feature of the politician like her type. In the context of the model of political selection already presented, such information would move the parameter G, which describes the electorate's average preference toward (or against) the incumbent. Specifically, the district-level preference bump enjoyed by the incumbent changes G to $G + \eta$, where $\eta < 0$ is associated with a negative scandal and $\eta > 0$ is associated with a positive bump, like a celebrity endorsement. We consider this alternative mechanism – voter preferences – as analogous to our model above from Chapter 2 where the only change is the content of the informational message.

If voter i does not receive the preference bump signal, she prefers the incumbent whenever

$$v_i + G + P(t_I = 1) \geq P(t_C = 1).$$

Since $P(t_I = 1) = P(t_C = 1) = q$, this reduces to $v_I \geq -G$. If instead, voter i receives the preference bump signal, then she prefers the incumbent whenever

$$v_i + G + \eta + P(t_I = 1) \geq P(t_C = 1),$$

which reduces to $v_i \geq -G - \eta$. Combining these, incumbent vote share is

$$V_\eta(\mu; G) = \mu(1 - F(-G - \eta)) + (1 - \mu)(1 - F(-G)).$$

Following logic similar to above, that is, that G varies across districts, the empirical target for the incumbent's vote share then becomes

$$(\mu'' - \mu') \mathbb{E}_G \left[\frac{dV_\eta(\mu; G)}{d\mu} \right].$$

Our model suggests that there are multiple mechanisms through which an informational campaign could affect the incumbent's vote share. Our principal example considers an adverse selection mechanism where signals provide information about the incumbent's type (or immutable characteristics). This secondary example suggests that information about a candidate that is unrelated to the candidate's type could change voters' preferences for the incumbent over the challenger. Postulating which mechanism(s) are activated by an intervention becomes crucial for evidence accumulation.

4.1.2 Qualitative versus Quantitative Relationships

When is it sensible to accumulate empirical findings from different studies and why? An answer to this question must address the relationship between empirical targets across studies. Recall that empirical targets are the quantitative object that define the effect of a mechanism relative to a research design, and that they are represented in setting θ by the treatment effect function, $\tau_m^\gamma(\omega', \omega'' \mid \theta)$, for measurement strategy m, contrast (ω', ω''), and evaluated at estimand γ. Implicit in this formulation is that the function $\tau_m^\gamma(\omega', \omega'' \mid \theta)$ reflects the influence of a single mechanism. The first problem that arises when looking at a meta-study of voter information interventions is that information interventions might activate different and distinct mechanisms. As a consequence, studies that have been brought together may lack a common conceptual foundation.

Both variants of the model provide a theoretical representation of the impact of an information treatment on the vote share of incumbents, which we express as empirical targets. Yet, the substantive mechanism that connects information manipulation with incumbent electoral success in each model is different. In one case, voters are responding to information about an incumbent's immutable characteristics which are relevant for future performance. In the other case, they are responding to information about their preference for candidates.

Typical statistical exercises require more than a qualitative relationship between empirical targets, they also need a *quantitative relationship* so that the resulting test reflects substantive features rather than artifacts of measurement or differences across features of research design. Using the expressions for the average treatment effect in each case, we can examine what can go wrong when the quantitative relationship between empirical targets is neglected.

Under what conditions does adverse selection and a voter preference bump produce equivalent empirical targets? For the empirical targets on vote share to be equivalent, we would need

$$\underbrace{(\mu'' - \mu')\mathbb{E}_G\left[\frac{dV_0(\mu; G)}{d\mu}\right]}_{\text{Adverse selection empirical target}} = \underbrace{(\mu'' - \mu')\mathbb{E}_G\left[\frac{dV_\eta(\mu; G)}{d\mu}\right]}_{\text{Voter preference bump empirical target}}. \tag{6}$$

The question is not whether these expressions are ever the same, because there is at least one value where they are, namely,

$$\eta = \frac{q(1-q)(1-2p)}{pq + (1-p)(1-q)}.$$

The question is whether these expressions are the same for a wide range of values of η. Put differently, are two harmonized experiments that differ only in the content of the message "likely" to produce the same empirical targets? Ultimately, the set where the two empirical targets, one for adverse selection and the other for a preference bump, are the same is so small that the probability of empirical targets being in that set is zero. The intuition is straightforward: The preference bump enjoyed by an incumbent has to exactly match the bump an incumbent receives from good news about her type. This kind of coincidence is exceedingly unlikely. Thus, even the harmonization of research designs cannot guarantee a quantitative equivalence between empirical targets absent theoretical considerations. The reason is that the exact mechanism underlying the empirical targets in each case is different (the function τ is different in each case). Consequently, ensuring alignment of the empirical targets is challenging. This example highlights the need to consider both qualitative and quantitative features of the cross-study environment when attempting to accumulate evidence.

4.2 Uniting Principle I: Common Concepts

The first uniting principle, **common concepts**, is relatively straightforward. It requires that a common mechanism exists and is thought to present across constituent studies. When Uniting Principle I is satisfied, a mechanism's influence can be described using the same terms and concepts. If there is no conceptual link between studies, then there is no basis for which comparing, combining, or extrapolating empirical targets can teach us anything about the generality of a mechanism or the attendant phenomena. For example, a meta-study of political accountability that includes at least one study examining the effect of information in the context of preference change, and at least one study examining the effect of adverse selection, will fail to identify anything clearly related to either mechanism. Such meta-studies are, at best, constrained to learning about the manipulation technology, here, providing information to voters, and answering whether voters respond to information rather than how or why voters respond to the information they are provided.

Common concepts are given by substantive arguments and cannot be fulfilled using statistical techniques. To illustrate, we conduct a meta-analysis of estimated treatment effects from two types of experiments. A meta-analysis *combines* estimates from multiple studies or samples to estimate parameter(s) that are common across the estimates from constituent studies. We discuss the specific meta-analytic estimands in depth in Chapter 5. In this meta-analysis, we will estimate (a) the mean of the distribution of treatment effects, and (b) a precision-weighted average of treatment effects.

In line with our running example on political selection, we will first consider a set of vignette survey experiments on corruption and support for incumbents compiled by Incerti (2020). In contrast to the case of good news about the incumbent that we have worked through, these experiments investigate the converse case of bad news: The signal suggests that the (hypothetical) incumbent is corrupt. Here, the treatment is a provision of a vignette with information that an incumbent has been found to be corrupt; the control instrument is typically a vignette without information about corruption.[11] We will examine the effects on individual vote intentions for the incumbent. Treatment effects can therefore be interpreted as the difference in probability of an intended vote for the incumbent when corruption is revealed versus when it is not revealed.

Second, we include ostensibly unrelated survey experiments that measure voter preferences for female (as opposed to male) candidates. Women are underrepresented in politics in most contexts and voter bias against female candidates is one potential explanation for this underrepresentation. Using conjoint or vignette experiments, researchers try to assess the degree to which survey respondents support female candidate profiles or vignettes under "all-else-equal" conditions. Schwarz and Coppock (2022) collect a set of experiments spanning the 1980s–2020s in a variety of national and subnational contexts. They report the average treatment effect of a "female" profile on the probability that the profile is chosen (typically out of two paired profiles). As a result, treatment effects can be interpreted as the difference in the probability of selection of female versus male candidates.

We report the estimated treatment effects and meta-analytic effects in Figure 1. In the top panel, it is clear that corruption revelations substantially depress vote intention for the incumbent. In the second panel, the effect of a female profile on vote intentions produces smaller and mostly positive effects. Pooling studies in both panels, we estimate the mean of the distribution of treatment effects to be -0.053 (or 5.3 percentage points) with a 95% confidence interval of $[-0.086, -0.021]$.[12] Indeed, we would reject the null hypothesis that the mean of the distribution of treatment effects is equivalent to zero at standard thresholds (here, $p < 0.01$).[13] Yet, this inference is nonsensical because the constituent studies have no apparent qualitative relationship to each other beyond the fact that both measure some type of vote intention. The experiments on accountability in the top panel report the effect of corruption

---

[11] As we note in some examples, the comparison of interest in the constituent survey experiments can vary.

[12] Our estimate is obtained from a random-effects meta-analysis estimator.

[13] With a fixed-effects meta-analysis estimator, we estimate a common effect of -0.002 (0.2 percentage points) with a 95% confidence interval of $[-0.003, -0.001]$), $p < 0.001$.

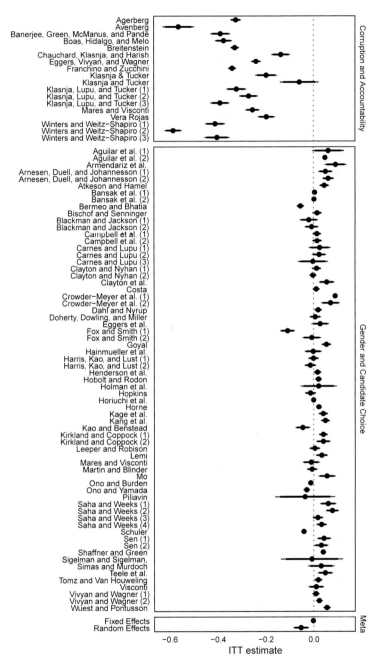

Figure 1 Meta-analysis of treatment effects from two sets of studies. All points are estimated intent-to-treat (ITT) effects. Thick segments are 90% confidence intervals and thin segments are 95% confidence intervals. Note that estimates from the studies of corruption and incumbent support come from an earlier meta-analysis by Incerti (2020) and the studies of gender and candidate choice come from an earlier meta-analysis by Schwarz and Coppock (2022).

information on incumbent vote share. The experiments on gender and candidate choice in the middle panel seek to estimate the effect of a profile's gender on the probability of selection of that profile. While both outcomes can be interpreted as probabilities, they correspond to different outcomes such that the meta-analytic estimate mixes different treatments and outcomes without any known mapping between them.

It is important to stress that this meta-analysis was conducted *without careful consideration of the underlying mechanisms or the cross-study environment*. We do this to show how theoretically underdeveloped meta-analyses provide estimates that have no claim of substantive or quantitative relevance. It is unclear how we would define a common mechanism, not least a common parameter – such as the population average treatment effect, or the mean of a distribution of treatment effects – that would project onto both sets of studies.

Our stylized meta-analysis of experiments on corruption and accountability, and on gender and candidate choice, shows that although it is possible to combine evidence collected in different settings, it is not always sensible to do so. Specifically, combining evidence is misleading when there is no theoretical rationale to unite these studies. Such a qualitative rationale would be needed to justify any interpretation of the quantitative meta-analytic estimate it produces. This observation may seem obvious, but only because we picked examples that were very clearly distinct.[14] Not all cases of evidence accumulation are so clear cut, which highlights the importance of being explicit and clear about what concepts are common between different constituent studies. Figure 1 does not represent a sensible effort to accumulate evidence. Importantly, these problems have nothing to do with our ability to actually estimate a common treatment effect. Indeed, with modern statistical software, it is straightforward to estimate either meta-analytic model provided a set of treatment effect estimates and associated standard errors from constituent studies. *The challenge of accumulating evidence has remarkably little to do with estimation.*

4.3 Uniting Principle II: Quantitative Connection

When constituent studies share a common conceptual framework, they are related qualitatively. Is this sufficient for the kind of statistical tests or other quantitative exercises that researchers may want to pursue? No. Even when focusing exclusively on information experiments that convey information about incumbents, there is no guarantee of a quantitative connection between studies.

---

[14] It is straightforward to come up with even sillier examples.

The second uniting principle, **quantitative connection**, requires specification of a deterministic quantitative relationship between empirical targets. It
is more subtle than the first uniting principle, but it is equally important. This
uniting principle requires that the concepts and structure uniting constituent
studies are formulated and measured in such a way as to make them quantitatively comparable. Without Uniting Principle II, the theoretical relationship
between empirical targets across studies is underspecified and vague. As a consequence, we cannot know whether different studies are speaking to the same
quantities – even if they speak to the same concepts.

The second uniting principle is about more than just the underlying concepts in each study – it is about the quantitative relationship between them.
The requirement that the empirical targets of different constituent studies are
related by some deterministic relationship is necessary for a meta-study to produce a quantitatively meaningful estimate, test, or other measure. Otherwise,
quantitative tools, such as statistical tests, are not applicable because they constitute quantitative evaluative criteria applied to objects that have – at best –
only a qualitative relationship.

We highlight the importance of having a quantitative relationship between
empirical targets by conducting a meta-analysis using the data by Incerti
(2020). Incerti (2020) stratifies corruption and accountability experiments into
survey and field experiments. What would happen if one pooled all of these estimates into a single meta-analytic model? In principle, these experiments satisfy
Uniting Principle I as they invoke the same mechanism: adverse selection.

Figure 2 reports meta-analytic estimates of the mean effects across the field
and survey experiments on corruption and accountability that were originally
assembled by Incerti (2020). The random-effects estimate of the mean of the
distribution of treatment effects is -0.215 (21.5 percentage points) with a 95%
confidence interval of $[-0.285, -0.144]$). The obvious disparity between the
survey and field experimental estimates – the primary result in Incerti (2020) –
suggests a large discrepancy between the two types of studies. What, then, is
this quantity?

To understand the meta-analytic estimate in Figure 2, consider more closely
what treatment effects are measured in the constituent studies. Here, we
compare features of the two constituent studies: one survey experiment,
Mares and Visconti (2020), and one field experiment, Chong et al. (2015). In a
conjoint survey fielded in Romania, Mares and Visconti (2020) randomly vary
whether a hypothetical candidate was found to be clean, investigated, or sentenced by an anti-corruption authority. The outcome is an indicator for whether

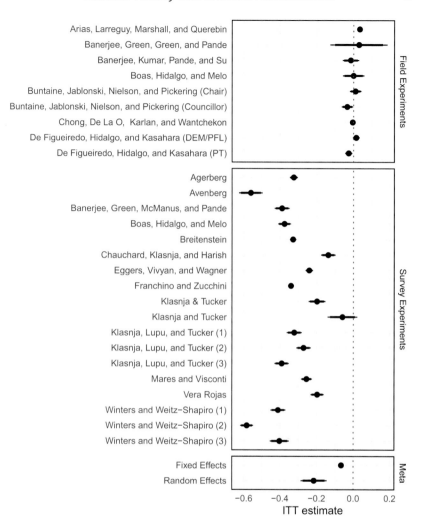

Figure 2 Meta-analysis of field and survey experiments on corruption and accountability. Thick segments are 90% confidence intervals and thin segments are 95% confidence intervals. The estimates come from an existing meta-analysis by Incerti (2020).

a hypothetical candidate profile was selected within a pair of candidates.[15] The estimated average treatment effect of corruption on vote choice of 25 percentage points in Incerti (2020) (and therefore Figure 2) comes from a specification that pools the "investigated" and "sentenced" levels into a single treatment and compares them to the "clean" (no irregularity) condition.

---

[15] This was not a forced-choice conjoint experiment, meaning that respondents could choose either or neither candidate.

In the other study, a field experiment conducted in 12 municipalities in Mexico, Chong et al. (2015) provide precincts of voters (clusters) with information about the results of a national government audit of the use of a sizable intergovernmental transfer to municipalities. In this sense, all municipalities in the sample were investigated in a previous year. The corruption information revealed the proportion of funds that were "spent with corruption" (Chong et al., 2015, pg. 59), which ranged from 1% (very limited corruption) to 100% (all spending was designated as corrupt) across municipalities in the sample. The authors compare the corruption information to placebo fliers that provide information about the intergovernmental transfer, but not corruption information. They find that relative to the placebo condition, corruption information reduces vote share for the incumbent party as a share of registered voters by 0.43 percentage points.

While these studies arguably seek to measure the effect of a similar mechanism, are these effects quantitatively comparable? First, consider the contrasts in each of the studies. The present analysis of the conjoint experiment compares vignettes "sentenced" or "investigated" for corruption to those that were investigated but found to be "clean." In this sense, the comparison is bad news (corruption) to good news (no corruption). The contrast in the field experiment, however, compares *any* information about corruption (which could be good or bad) to no information about corruption in the placebo condition. These comparisons are clearly different and there is not an obvious reason that we should expect them to produce the same effect.

Second, the outcome measurement strategies are very different. The outcomes in the conjoint survey ask respondents to choose one of two hypothetical candidates or neither. Choosing a candidate – which is, in principle, analogous to voting – does not have a cost in this survey setting. In contrast, in the field setting, there are three important distinctions. First, because consecutive re-election was prohibited, the authors focus on votes for the incumbent *party*, not a specific candidate. Second, voting has costs in the field setting and there are arguably stakes to voters' choices in elections. Finally, in Mexico's multi party elections, voters generally have more than two candidates to choose from. In the placebo control group, just 17.2% of registered voters (or 33.0% of voters) selected the incumbent party. Even though both studies seek to evaluate a similar mechanism, they do so using wildly different research designs.

These studies represent just two component studies of the meta-analysis in Figure 2. Can the meta-analyst overcome the idiosyncratic choices that go into individual studies by evaluating a weighted average of study estimates as in our random- and fixed-effects estimates? Averaging empirical targets without a quantitative connection – where Uniting Principle II fails – cannot recover a meaningful quantity, and thus does not produce substantively meaningful information about the application at hand. In this case, adding additional studies on a mechanism, as in Figure 2, does not make the average any more interpretable. If anything, it further complicates our understanding of the meta-estimand.

4.4 Summing Up

Uniting principles are about the relationship across and between studies. They present concerns that are separate and orthogonal to within-study issues like identification, estimation, or commensurability (Ashworth et al., 2021; Bueno de Mesquita & Tyson, 2020). However, we cannot accumulate evidence from multiple studies without knowledge of how these studies are related to each other qualitatively and quantitatively. Consequently, accumulating evidence is necessarily less "agnostic" than is possible in the case of a single study. While every example using a meta-study (e.g., replication, meta-analysis, etc.) necessarily invokes a set of uniting principles, the principles are rarely formulated or made explicit. Omissions of this kind thus create problems because they leave the scope of the cross-study environment, and the subsequent interpretation of a meta-study's findings, ambiguous and potentially misleading.

Our discussion has focused on two uniting principles, illustrated with stylized models and purposefully flawed meta-analyses that highlight their importance. Uniting Principle I is about qualitative equivalence and holds that constituent studies be about common concepts. It is illustrated by the meta-analysis in Figure 1, which combines candidate gender and corruption experiments. That analysis lacked an argument for a common – or even closely related – mechanism, and without such an argument, the common (hyper)parameter that we estimated, the mean of the distribution of ITTs, lacked any substantive meaning. Uniting Principle II – quantitative connection – requires a deterministic quantitative relationship between empirical targets, which is about a mechanism and a research design. The second uniting principle is illustrated by the meta-analysis in Figure 2, where there is (arguably) a compelling argument that the authors are measuring the effect of a common mechanism in different settings. However, in this case, the design differences across studies lead to study estimates that lack a quantitative relationship. Measuring the effect of the same mechanism in different ways can undermine the interpretation of a common parameter, in much the same way as when common concepts are lacking. Consequently, the meta-analytic estimate reported in Figure 2 is comprised of a vague combination of different things.

Readers may be tempted to address failures of the first uniting principle – common concepts – by redefining concepts. In our stylized example, suppose a researcher were confronted with one experiment that measures the effect of adverse selection and another that measures the effect of voter preferences. The researcher may be tempted to justify accumulation efforts by saying that both studies consider the effect of a message that is provided to voters. This is akin to saying that the studies share a common – albeit redefined – concept. But even in this simple case, ensuring a quantitative connection between empirical targets would require more than simple harmonization of research designs. It would also require aspects of the empirical target that depend on how a mechanism is expressed to also be the same. By abstracting from the mechanisms thought to be at work, researchers make it more difficult to justify a quantitative relationship between studies.

None of the issues in our discussion nor the meta-analyses we conduct in this section are indicative of weaknesses of the constituent studies. Instead, the lack of clear uniting principles are what make the results of the meta-studies suspect, because uniting principles are only about the relationship between studies. Moreover, this analysis suggests that the accumulation of evidence from multiple studies requires additional considerations, and that the uniting principles we highlight should guide those considerations.

PART II: APPLICATIONS

We now shift our attention from the broad concepts that are important to understanding evidence accumulation to assess three of the most common tools used to measure or evaluate the generalizability of social phenomena. We focus on the uniting principles invoked by each application.

Existing guidance on external validity and evidence accumulation generally follows one of two paths. The first path involves **gathering**, advocating to "do more studies," or gather the findings across credible studies in multiple samples or contexts (Banerjee & Duflo, 2009; Dunning, 2016). This path is evident in both replication and meta-analysis. It is characteristic of individual replication studies as well as larger multi-study replication efforts across the social sciences (e.g., Camerer et al., 2016, 2018; Open Science Collaboration, 2015). The push to "do more studies" is evident in Evidence in Governance and Politics' Metaketa initiative (Blair et al., 2021; de la O et al., 2021; Dunning et al., 2019a; Slough et al., 2021). A second approach to causal generalization focuses on **extrapolation**, where empirical effects in one setting (or for a population) are constructed from empirical findings measured in other places. Approaches focusing on extrapolation to other samples emphasize the reweighting of various findings to samples of units or contexts with different covariate profiles (Cole & Stuart, 2010; Egami & Hartman, 2023; Kern et al., 2016; Pearl & Bareinboim, 2011, 2014).

Both the gathering and extrapolation approaches invoke distinct – and often implicit – uniting principles. There are multiple ways that one can engage in evidence generalization quantitatively, and we focus on the three most common approaches: combining, comparing, and extrapolating. First, meta-analysis, across its various forms, represents an effort to *combine* evidence, taking as an input data or estimates from a collection of multiple studies that are united by a common structure. This structure makes assumptions about the relationship between the empirical targets in multiple studies. We make explicit these assumptions in order to better understand the relationship between external validity and meta-analytic methods.

Second, replication is an exercise in *comparison* of study results. Furthermore, the same logic that goes into formally comparing studies can be found more broadly in less formal efforts to aggregate findings. For example, when researchers in a single-setting study contextualize their estimates to related findings in the literature, they engage in similar, albeit informal, comparisons. Accumulation through comparison requires at least two studies that measure a given effect.

Third, some methods for causal generalization rely on treatment effect estimates from a single study to *extrapolate* treatment effects in a grand population or another setting. Extrapolating differs from comparing or combining because it typically requires only a single study as an input.[16] Consequently, while the comparing and combining approaches involve a meta-study, extrapolating does not. Extrapolation-based approaches have been the subject of more recent *statistical* developments relative to comparison- or combination-based approaches. However, these methods are not yet widely utilized in applied work. We summarize these three approaches to accumulation of evidence in Table 2, highlighting each approach with several examples.

Running Application

Throughout the next three chapters, we focus on two of the six Metaketa-I experiments on voter information and electoral accountability because the efforts to harmonize ex-ante represent current best practices for evidence accumulation. Specifically, we discuss the experiments in Brazil and Mexico. By focusing on two Metaketa experiments, we examine two experiments where

---

[16] Note that these methods are typically validated using existing meta-studies for which there are estimates from multiple settings.

Table 2 Three approaches to evidence generalization

Chapter	Approach	Research design	Meta-study?	Applied Examples
5	Combining	Meta-analysis	✓	Banerjee et al. (2015); Blair et al. (2021); Dunning et al. (2019a); Slough et al. (2021)
6	Comparing	Replication (direct or conceptual)	✓	Camerer et al. (2018); Open Science Collaboration (2015); Raffler et al. (2020)
7	Extrapolating	(No standardized name)	–	Dehejia et al. (2021)

there was some ex-ante coordination/harmonization across teams, as documented in Dunning et al. (2019b). While these studies have already been included in a meta-analysis reported in Dunning et al. (2019a), we use this opportunity to discuss the underlying assumptions of meta-analysis with respect to these studies and to compare and contrast meta-analysis to the other methods we present.

To provide context for our running application, in the past two decades, a number of Latin American governments, including those of Brazil and Mexico, have adopted some form of audits of intergovernmental transfers to local governments. In the course of these audits, national or state bureaucrats audit the accounts of municipal governments in search of corruption or misuse of funds. These audits provide a measure of an incumbent's corruption and have inspired a large body of literature. The field experiments we discuss develop campaigns to disseminate audit results prior to local elections. These interventions allow for measurement of how voters respond to revelations of corruption (or lack thereof) when they cast their ballots.

The first study considers information and accountability in the Northeastern Brazilian state of Pernambuco. In the field experimental component of the project, survey enumerators disseminated fliers that communicated the results of the audit (account accepted or rejected) with voters. This flier was distributed at the conclusion of a baseline survey. This intervention was randomized at the individual level, meaning that there is within-municipality variation in the information assigned to voters. They measure outcomes at the individual level in a post-election survey. The primary outcome of interest in the experiment, which we analyze, is self-reported vote choice for the incumbent.

The second study examined information and accountability in 26 municipalities across four states in Mexico (Arias et al. 2022). In the field experiment, an NGO disseminated leaflets describing the use or misuse of federal funds in their municipalities. The information treatment contained four variants, though we follow the original researchers by collapsing over these treatment variants. The treatments were cluster-assigned at the precinct level. To maintain closer harmonization with the Brazil study, we will focus on survey-measured vote choice for the incumbent party (as Mexican mayors are limited to one consecutive term).

We will stratify on the content of the signal, as in our running example from the first part (Concepts). While there is not a direct mapping between the audit results in the two contexts, we make a qualitative distinction between an objectively "good" audit outcome for the mayor and a (potentially) "bad" audit outcome. In Brazil, following Boas et al. (2019), we distinguish municipalities with approved versus rejected accounts. In Mexico, we distinguish municipalities for which no misuse of funds was detected in the ASF audit from those that detected misuse of the funds. We note that "approved accounts" and "no misuse" are the modal audit outcomes in both settings. Indeed, both experiments oversample municipalities where corruption was detected. We depict the distribution of both municipalities and respondents in each experimental sample in each of these two categories in Table 3.

We use these studies to describe meta-analysis, replication, and extrapolation-based research designs. It is useful to present a single example to understand how these designs relate to each other. However, the use of coordinated studies has features that contrast with the modal uses of these designs in the literature. First, most meta-analyses are retrospective compilations of studies that were conducted without any coordination between scholars or prior planning. We argue that the prospective coordination and attempt to harmonize the Brazil and Mexico experiments represents an advance in meta-analytic practice. Taking advantage of the coordination of these studies allows us to most

Table 3 No corruption refers to "accounts accepted" in Brazil and no detected corruption in Mexico. All data come from replication packages from Dunning et al. (2019b), Boas et al. (2019), and Arias et al. (2022). 95% confidence intervals are reported in brackets

Share of	Brazil	Mexico
Respondents in municipalities without corruption	0.503 [0.482, 0.525]	0.464 [0.451, 0.478]
Municipalities in sample without corruption	0.848 [0.740, 0.955]	0.461 [0.256, 0.667]

clearly articulate the uniting principles invoked in meta-analyses. Retrospective meta-analyses are *easier* to criticize on these grounds. Consequently, our selection of these studies forces us to be more specific in our discussion.

Second, some readers may object to the use of two studies that were developed concurrently to discuss replication. Replication designs often consist of an "original" study and a "replication" study at a later date. Does this distinction matter? As we note in Chapter 6, replications can be used for multiple purposes. When used to evaluate the generality of a mechanism in multiple settings, the original and replication studies are typically treated symmetrically when subjected to formal statistical tests. In other words, the order of the studies is not material to the analysis. Outside the context of assessments of external validity, replication can also be used to describe characteristics of a substantive literature (e.g., Camerer et al., 2016; Open Science Collaboration, 2015). For this use of replication, some diagnostic assessments of issues related to research practices rely on the order of studies. Since our focus is on the former use of replication to assess the generality of a mechanism, the use of two concurrent studies allows us to illustrate the use of replication studies for this purpose.

5 Meta-analysis

The first method for evidence accumulation we examine is *meta-analysis*, which *combines* the estimates from two or more studies conducted on multiple samples or in different settings. The central output of a meta-analysis is some summary of the set of estimates, and different meta-analytic models estimate different summary quantities or parameters.

Most meta-analyses are retrospective and conduct secondary analysis of existing studies. For example, the Schwarz and Coppock (2022) and Incerti (2020) meta-analyses that we discussed in Chapter 4 collect and then synthesize existing studies (published or unpublished). This design is widespread in education, psychology, and medicine. A critical design decision in such retrospective meta-analyses is defining the inclusion criteria for studies. As we discussed in our "non-sensical" meta-analysis in Chapter 4, the inclusion of studies that measure the effects of different mechanisms results in an output that lacks any quantitative meaning or interpretability. While the vast majority of meta-analyses are retrospective, a growing number of prospective meta-analyses have been conducted in political science and economics. In these studies, multiple RCTs are designed and implemented in coordination with an eye toward a formal synthesis. EGAP's Metaketa project has facilitated five of these studies to date, of which four are complete (Blair et al., 2021; de la O et al., 2021; Dunning et al., 2019a; Slough et al., 2021). Similar designs have also been utilized outside the Metaketas, for example, by Banerjee et al. (2015) and Coppock et al. (2020). These studies come closest to the design-driven approach that we advocate.

5.1 The Challenge of Combining Estimates

Why do researchers seek to combine estimates from multiple studies through a meta-analysis? Some authors explicitly cite learning about the generalizability – or external validity – of a particular causal mechanism (or its effect). For the purposes of conceptual clarity, and before we proceed to a more detailed discussion of actual models, consider a stripped-down example of a meta-analysis of two studies. Take two constituent studies, 1 and 2, that are designed to study the influence of a single common mechanism. Suppose further that in the settings where studies 1 and 2 were conducted, the common mechanism is the only mechanism capable of generating the observed effects, that is, there are no additional mechanisms or mediators present.

The measured treatment effects in studies 1 and 2 are h_1 and h_2, respectively, and for the purposes of our example, suppose these effects are measured absent statistical noise.[17] Because of the single common mechanism producing the treatment effects, we have fulfilled our first uniting principle. How should one think about the second uniting principle? We might imagine that the effects in each study can be written as

$$h_1 = H + \kappa_1 \quad \text{and} \quad h_2 = H + \kappa_2, \tag{7}$$

where H is the common effect that we are interested in measuring, and κ_1 and κ_2 capture differences between the observed effects resulting from differences in research design. Under these assumptions, h_1 and h_2 are the empirical targets of studies 1 and 2, respectively.

Since the most common meta-analytic estimands can be characterized as a weighted average of estimates from constituent studies, we can write the empirical target of the meta-analysis as

$$\alpha h_1 + (1 - \alpha)h_2,$$

where the respective weights on the two studies are $\alpha \in (0, 1)$ and $1 - \alpha$.[18] By substitution, this means that the empirical target of the meta-analysis is

$$H + \underbrace{\alpha\kappa_1 + (1 - \alpha)\kappa_2}_{B}.$$

---

[17] One could suppose that both hypothetical studies have an infinite sample size.
[18] After normalization, the assumption that $\alpha \in (0, 1)$ is without loss of generality.

Thus, the empirical target of the meta-analysis is the combination of empirical targets from studies 1 and 2. When $h_1 \neq h_2$, the empirical targets of studies 1 and 2 are not the same, and thus, $B \neq 0$. Without statistical noise, there are no statistical reasons that the observed effects between studies 1 and 2 differ, and since there is only the common mechanism in studies 1 and 2, B cannot be the result of an additional mechanism (or mediator) present in one of the studies. In what ways can this quantity be used to make an inference about the external validity of the mechanism? For most analysts, this question ultimately reduces to measuring the value of H. In this section, we will show that such statements about external validity are misleading because the standard models used to conduct meta-analysis *assume* the external validity of the underlying mechanism – through Uniting Principle II.

5.2 Uniting Principles

The uniting principles invoked in meta-analysis are typically formulated by the statistical model used to conduct the meta-analysis and are rarely stated explicitly. In this section, we uncover the uniting principles that underlie common approaches to meta-analysis to better understand the relationship between meta-analysis and evidence accumulation.

From our simple example above, the uniting principles of a meta-analysis model that posits the relationship in (7) follow from assumptions about H and B. Here, the *assumed existence of a common effect*, H, serves as the principle that unites studies 1 and 2, thus completing Uniting Principle I. Moreover, Uniting Principle II is satisfied by the assumption that treatment effects can be written as $h_i = H + \kappa_i$ for $i = 1, 2$, specifying the quantitative relationship between studies 1 and 2 through their relationship to the quantity H.[19]

Researchers invoke a number of statistical assumptions when they conduct a meta-analysis. These statistical assumptions are needed to address issues (e.g., sampling variability) that, by assumption, do not arise in our simple example. However, in some cases, these statistical assumptions do more than address statistical issues – they also *impose* uniting principles. To see this, suppose that we were to invoke a standard statistical assumption in our example. Specifically, suppose that all deviations from H, even though no statistical issues are present, are nevertheless representable as random noise that has zero mean. Consequently, κ_1 and κ_2 are independent draws from some mean-zero distribution, essentially making them equivalent to statistical noise. This is a standard implication of meta-analysis models that impose ancillary statistical assumptions that indirectly address the B term from our example.

---

[19] Specifically, by substitution, $h_1 = h_2 - \kappa_2 + \kappa_1$.

The two workhorse statistical models for meta-analysis, the fixed- and random-effects models, effectively discard B by assuming that it is random, mean-zero, noise. Importantly, the assumption that B is structurally equivalent to statistical noise is a theoretical assumption that forms part of Uniting Principle II. In such cases, the statistical structure of the meta-analysis model implies theoretical and substantive content. By showing explicitly the link between uniting principles and these statistical assumptions, we show how the statistical model imposes additional theoretical assumptions about the cross-study structure of a meta-analysis.

We have asserted that Uniting Principle II is often implicit in standard practice. How, then, are the uniting principles typically addressed? For retrospective meta-analyses, the PRISMA protocols are widely used in systematic reviews and meta-analysis. These protocols provide guidance for search/inclusion criteria for retrospective meta-analyses across disciplines (Moher et al., 2015). They require reporting of inclusion (eligibility) criteria, data items (e.g., variables), and outcomes to be included in a meta-analysis or systematic review. These features constrain, to some degree, the relationship between constituent studies or estimates. Although the PRISMA protocols are the closest thing to an explicit treatment of uniting principles, they are qualitative suggestions, and thus only address Uniting Principle I (at best).

Prospective meta-analyses (like the Metaketas) address (portions of) the uniting principles through the selection of study settings and the design of constituent studies. In particular, researchers typically select settings where a common mechanism could theoretically arise, addressing Uniting Principle I. Moreover, efforts to harmonize interventions and measurement strategies endeavor to reduce the possibility that differences in effects are driven by differences in research designs, thus making important advances toward Uniting Principle II. However, they are not sufficient to ensure a quantitative relationship between empirical targets without further invocation of external validity. As such, in both prospective and retrospective meta-analyses, Uniting Principle II is widely assumed, but rarely justified.

5.2.1 Meta-analytic Models: The Random-Effects Model

There are two workhorse models used in most meta-analysis applications: the fixed-effects and the random-effects models. In this section, we consider the random-effects model because it is currently more common in social science applications and because the fixed-effects model can be motivated as a special case of the random-effects model.

When applied to meta-analysis, one supposes that each constituent study, indexed by i, produces an empirical target, $\tau_{mj}^{i,\gamma_j}(\omega_j', \omega_j'' \mid \theta_j)$, which is independent of θ_j because the setting's effect on the empirical target will be modeled as random noise. In its most basic form, the cross-study environment is captured by a model with two levels:

$$\beta^i_{m_j}(\omega'_j, \omega''_j) = \lambda_i + u_i,$$
$$\lambda_i = \tau^{i,\gamma_j}_{m_j}(\omega'_j, \omega''_j) + \varepsilon_i. \tag{8}$$

The random-effects model exhibits statistical noise at each level, where u_i represents statistical noise within study i, and ε_i represents statistical noise arising from the sampling of constituent study settings. Here, $\beta^i_{m_j}(\omega'_j, \omega''_j)$ measures the empirical target, $\tau^{i,\gamma_j}_{m_j}(\omega'_j, \omega''_j)$, by producing an estimate of the treatment effect in constituent study i.

The random-effects model follows only after two additional assumptions about the cross-study environment. One details the statistical structure of the noise terms, and the other specifies the ontological and quantitative relationship between studies.

Assumption 1 *The study-specific error, u_i, is drawn across i from a normal distribution with mean 0 and variance σ^2, and the mean-level random error, ε_i, is drawn across i from a normal distribution with mean 0 and variance v^2.*

The error terms within constituent studies, u_i, as they manifest in the random-effects model, are meant to capture things like sampling variability, chance imbalances in the assignment of the instruments, or random measurement error that manifests within each individual study. The other error terms between constituent studies, ε_i, represent differences in the means between studies that can be attributed to random factors across i.

For identification in the random-effects model, an additional assumption is required. Without positing further structure on the random-effects model, the empirical targets, $\tau^{i,\gamma_j}_{m_j}(\omega'_j, \omega''_j)$, need not be the same across constituent studies, i. It is precisely this feature that uniting principles are meant to deal with. This leads to the second assumption underlying the use of the random-effects model for meta-analysis, which asserts a quantitative relationship between empirical targets across constituent studies.

Assumption 2 (Design Invariance) *There is an underlying structural parameter, $T \in \mathbb{R}$, that is constant across studies, that is,*

$$T \equiv \tau^{i,\gamma}_m(\omega', \omega''),$$

for all i, all measurement strategies, $m \in M$, and all contrasts, $(\omega', \omega'') \in C$.

This assumption has two parts. The first posits the existence of a common parameter that unites all the constituent studies. This, along with the inclusion criteria determining which studies have this common parameter, fulfills Uniting Principle I in the case of meta-analysis. Specifically, it links the constituent studies through their relationship to T.

The second part of Assumption 2 fulfills Uniting Principle II, by positing that the mechanism being studied is not just common across studies but also that the effect of the common mechanism is *quantitatively the same across studies*. This implies that the mechanism produces exactly the same treatment effect in every study regardless of how it is observed (if it could be observed without error). In particular, it holds that treatment effects are invariant to the outcomes measured or the comparisons made. This invariance assumption implies that all treatment effects are equivalent to T, even when measurement strategies, m_j, and contrasts, (ω_j', ω_j''), differ across studies.

Design invariance is an explicit rejection of measurement perspectivism, as presented in Chapter 2. In particular, measurement perspectivism supposes that a mechanism's influence, when measured quantitatively, depends on how it is measured. This implies that the treatment effects across two studies differ when their research designs are not the same. In conjunction with the hierarchical structure in (8), design invariance implies a projectivist formulation of external validity (see Chapter 3). The notion that the parameter T is equivalent across studies, but that it may be observed with different levels of random error, is equivalent to formulating that the effect observed in constituent study i, $\beta_{m_j}^i(\omega_j', \omega_j'')$, is a projection from the common effect, T. The purpose, then, of the random-effects model is to identify the source, T, using the observed destinations as data.

Since Assumption 2 implicitly serves as Uniting Principle II for most meta-analyes that use a random-effects model, and because uniting principles reflect theoretical commitments, it is worth considering what commitments are being expressed by design invariance. To illustrate this, we employ the T-validity and Y-validity concepts from Egami and Hartman (2023). T-validity refers to the extent to which the assigned treatment (single study) and target treatment induce the same individual treatment effects (defined in terms of potential outcomes), and "T-bias is zero when the treatment-variation is irrelevant to treatment effects," which is reflected by Egami and Hartman (2023, Assumption 2, p. 10). Similarly, Y-validity applies when individual treatment effects are equivalent in the experiment and the target population, and "Y-bias is zero when the outcome-variation is irrelevant to treatment effects" (Egami & Hartman, 2023, p. 11). It is straightforward to show that, in the context of the random-effects model, T-validity and Y-validity are jointly equivalent to design invariance.

Now take, for example, a drug trial looking to measure the effect of insulin lispro. In most cases, insulin's influence is expected to depend on its dosage (the contrast). This constitutes a violation of *T*-validity. Similarly, assessing the effect of insulin lispro using a mortality indicator, instead of blood sugar (perhaps obtained via a finger stick), is not expected to produce the same quantitative effect, and this constitutes a violation of *Y*-validity. Design invariance thus theoretically *presumes* that features of the research design, like contrasts and measurement strategies, cannot influence the effect that is observed. In this way the random-effects model for meta-analysis dramatically limits the scope for credible evidence accumulation.

5.2.2 Other Meta-analytic Models

Although we have devoted attention to the random-effects model, we briefly discuss the other kinds of models that are commonly applied to meta-analysis. First, we consider the fixed-effects meta-analysis model, the other workhorse model for meta-analysis. The fixed-effects model is a special case of (8), where $E[u_i] = 0$, $Var[u_i] = 0$, and $E[\varepsilon] = 0$ replace Assumption 1 to detail the statistical structure. Then, (8), under Assumption 2, simplifies to

$$\beta^i_{m_j}(\omega'_j, \omega''_j) = \tau^{i,\gamma_j}_{m_j}(\omega'_j, \omega''_j) + \varepsilon_i$$
$$= T + \varepsilon_i. \tag{9}$$

As in the random-effects model, the assertion of a common parameter – by design invariance – serves as the relevant uniting principle.

Second, note that the fixed-effects meta-analysis model in (9) can be represented as a precision-weighted average of estimated treatment effects.[20] Although the term "precision-weighted average" may seem to suggest less structure than our discussion of a common parameter, in the random effects model, (9) shows that the fixed-effects model similarly assumes a common parameter. Consequently, this approach does not constitute an alternative to formulating uniting principles. Ultimately, the very uniting principles that assert a common parameter are those that provide a meaningful interpretation of the meta-estimand in a fixed-effects meta-analysis.

Third, some meta-analytic models adopt deeper *l*-level structures where $l > 2$, which are more general formulations of the standard random-effects

---

[20] Denoting the estimated standard error on each estimate, $\beta^i_{m_j}(\omega'_j, \omega''_j)$, by σ_{β_i}, then an estimator of pooled (common) treatment effect in a fixed-effects model is

$$\frac{1}{\sum_i \sigma^2_{\beta_i}} \sum_i \frac{\beta^i_{m_j}(\omega'_j, \omega''_j)}{\sigma^2_{\beta_i}}.$$

model (e.g., Cheung, 2014). A unifying feature of these models is that level l contains a parameter that is common across the entire set of estimates, just as in the random-effects model.[21] This common parameter entails design invariance (Assumption 2) at the nth level, and hence, such models employ the same uniting principles as above. Thus, our discussion of the uniting principles of the random-effects model applies also to more general hierarchical models.

Fourth, most meta-regression models do not assume a common treatment effect across studies. Instead, in meta-regression, the sources of heterogeneity in treatment effects are explicitly modeled, and a vector of parameters are linked together through the model of the cross-study environment and heterogeneity of effects. The model and parameters constitute the fulfillment of Uniting Principle II. Meta-regression is a model-based approach since researchers rely on a model of the relationship between study design and measured treatment effects, or otherwise express their expectations about variation in the mechanisms that are activated across constituent studies. Learning from meta-regression, thus, relies on researchers' ability to model these features accurately.

5.2.3 Target-Equivalence

Ultimately, the random-effects model is just a model, and it is not tied to the abuse it expedites among practitioners. In particular, the theoretical commitments associated with design invariance often lack a clear substantive argument, and consequently, Assumption 2 is not generally satisfied in a wide array of applications.[22] What, then, is the alternative to design invariance that nevertheless facilitates use of the random-effects model?

The cross-sectionalist formulation of external validity provides a useful way to reconceptualize the random-effects model when applied to meta-analysis. To see how, note from our simple example, why is it important, theoretically, for $B = 0$? When $B \neq 0$, studies 1 and 2 do not have the same empirical target. Thus, B is *an artifact of non-random discrepancies in measurement or comparison.* Our example provides an important illustration of what can go awry when researchers combine studies that are "shooting at different targets."

The notion of "shooting at the same target" proves to be critical in meta-analysis. Recall that a single constituent study, $\mathcal{E}_i$, is comprised of a setting θ_i,

---

[21] Note that one common use of n-level models is to allow for a within-study variance component when analyzing multiple estimates from the same study, as in Godefroidt (2023). For this reason, we use "estimates" rather than "studies" as the unit of observation in this discussion.

[22] To see why this is the case, suppose that we are measuring an average treatment effect (ATE). We expect that if we were to reverse-code the treatment indicator, such that we have $t^i_{m_j}(\omega'_j, \omega''_j) = -t^i_{m_j}(\omega''_j, \omega'_j)$. For any $t^i_{m_j}(\omega'_j, \omega''_j) \neq 0$, design invariance fails.

a measurement strategy, m_i, and a contrast or comparison of interest, (ω_i', ω_i''). Recall also that the empirical target in study i is a function of these three ingredients and is denoted by the function $\tau_{m_i}^{\gamma_i}(\omega_i', \omega_i'' \mid \theta_i)$. What matters for meta-analysis is ensuring that these targets across i are the same.

Target-equivalence

Constituent studies, $\mathcal{E}_1 = \{m_1, (\omega_1', \omega_1''), \theta_1\}$ and $\mathcal{E}_2 = \{m_2, (\omega_2', \omega_2''), \theta_2\}$, are **target-equivalent** if

$$\tau_{m_1}^{\gamma_1}(\omega_1', \omega_1'' \mid \theta_1) = \tau_{m_2}^{\gamma_2}(\omega_2', \omega_2'' \mid \theta_2).$$

A meta-study has **target-equivalence** if all constituent studies i in $\mathcal{M}(\mathcal{I})$ are target-equivalent.

By inspecting the definition of target-equivalence, we can see that it involves both the external validity of treatment effects and the research design that is used to measure these effects. External validity is involved because we are measuring treatment effects across two different settings, θ_1 and θ_2, and it specifies how the empirical target, $\tau_m(\omega', \omega'' \mid \theta)$, changes over settings, θ. Features of the research design used in studies are also relevant because the empirical target changes with the measurement strategies, m, and contrasts, (ω', ω'').

Slough and Tyson (2023, Theorem 3) prove that *harmonization*, when the research designs are the same across i, and *exact external validity*, when the empirical target is constant in setting, are jointly necessary and sufficient for target-equivalence. This means that when a mechanism has exact external validity, a lack of harmonization implies that the empirical targets across studies are not the same.

When applied to the random-effects model, the cross-sectionalist formulation of external validity makes target-equivalence the core ingredient. Formally,

Assumption 3 *For any constituent study,* $\mathcal{E}_j = \{m_j, (\omega_j', \omega_j''), \theta_j\}$, *such that* $m_j = m$, *and* $(\omega_j', \omega_j'') = (\omega', \omega'')$, *the empirical target* $\tau_{m_j}(\omega_j', \omega_j'' \mid \theta_j)$ *is equal to* $\tau_m^{\gamma_i}(\omega', \omega'' \mid \theta)$, *that is,*

$$\beta_{m_j}^i(\omega_j', \omega_j'') = \tau_m^{\gamma_i}(\omega', \omega'' \mid \theta).$$

Slough and Tyson (2023, Proposition 2) show that this assumption, in conjunction with Assumption 1, is sufficient for identification in the random-effects model. Assumption 3 takes target-equivalence, which is necessary for meta-analysis, as the primary concept used to build uniting principles. How does Assumption 3 reflect the two uniting principles. First, Uniting Principle I is fulfilled through the inclusion criteria that go into putting constituent studies together. Second, Uniting Principle II is fulfilled by harmonization across studies. Specifically, because empirical targets differ in research designs, inclusion in a meta-analysis of only harmonized studies ensures that empirical targets can only differ in the extent to which they satisfy external validity.

Target-equivalence, where harmonization and exact external validity serve as uniting principles, may be considered too stringent, especially because ensuring harmonization can be extremely difficult in practice. How does target-equivalence, that is, Assumption 3, compare to design invariance, that is, Assumption 2? Note that design invariance implies target-equivalence, since Assumption 2 implies that the empirical targets are identical across constituent studies, regardless of whether harmonization holds. It is straightforward to see that target-equivalence does not logically imply design invariance, and as a consequence, Assumption 3 is logically weaker than what is typically invoked when applying the random-effects model to meta-analysis. What this says is that target-equivalence is less stringent than design invariance.

While target-equivalence may seem stringent, Slough and Tyson (2023) clarify that researchers have substantial control over the harmonization of studies – one necessary condition for target-equivalence – when they design a meta-study. Design invariance instead addresses these important design considerations through an assertion that such design differences do not matter. The logical relationship between target-equivalence and design invariance stresses the stringency in the relationship between empirical targets across settings when invoking the standard interpretation of the random-effects model. Any application of the random-effects meta-analysis model invokes identification assumptions, whether they are made explicit or not. Target-equivalence provides identification with less stringent theoretical commitments.

The necessity of harmonization for target-equivalence speaks to the benefits of prospective over retrospective meta-analyses. In prospective meta-analyses, like the Metaketas, and other studies like Banerjee et al. (2015) and Coppock et al. (2020), researchers aim to harmonize the design of the studies ex ante. While there are some practical limits to harmonization in this context—for example, status quo control conditions – it is far more likely that researchers can harmonize studies when they plan multiple studies from the outset than when they are sifting the literature for related studies. To this end, prospective meta-analyses represent a rare but important advance in meta-analytic practice.

5.3 External Validity and Meta-analysis

We indicated earlier that some authors view meta-analysis as a way to learn about the external validity of a mechanism. However, as we argue in the previous section, when identifying the common parameter, T, in a random-effects or fixed-effects meta-analysis model, researchers *assume* that the mechanism is (a) common across constituent studies, and (b) produces the same quantitative effect (i.e., is externally valid according to Definition 5). Consequently, external validity should be viewed as an *assumption facilitating meta-analysis*, rather than something that could be learned from a meta-analysis. Put differently, whatever information about external validity that may be contained in the estimates from constituent studies, using a meta-analysis is simply unable to provide information about it without begging the question.

Different uniting principles often constitute different formulations of external validity. We discussed above how the typical approach to meta-analysis, the random-effects model, uses design invariance (Assumption 2) as a uniting principle, which is consistent with a projective formulation of external validity. In particular, the common parameter, T, is the source, and the observed effects, which are the estimates combined in the meta-analysis, are the set of destinations. A meta-analysis treats the set of destinations, then, as the data that is put into the statistical model.

Cross-sectionalist formulations of external validity arguably apply more naturally to meta-analysis, because meta-analysis treats constituent studies symmetrically and need not impose a hierarchical structure upon them. This mirrors exactly how cross-sectionalism approaches external validity, without the need of an abstract source. Since meta-analysis requires target-equivalence, that is, a mechanism produces the same effect across settings, it requires exact external validity as formalized in Chapter 3. Important differences between targets emerge depending on the importance of research design (measurement strategies and contrasts) in producing treatment effects. Other cross-sectional versions of external validity, like sign-congruent external validity, do not facilitate target-equivalence, and are thus not appropriate for meta-analysis.

Finally, we emphasize that projective and cross-sectional formulations of external validity are not inconsistent with each other. Specifically, it is generally possible to connect cross-sectional with projective forms of external validity, in particular, because projective formulations are more stringent than cross-sectionalist formulations. This simply reflects that the uniting principles employed in most applications of the random-effects model are considerably stronger than what is necessary for meta-analysis.

5.4 The Value of Meta-analytic Estimates

It is important to note that meta-analysis can be a very useful method for evidence accumulation even if we cannot use it to learn about external validity. Setting aside misunderstandings about meta-analysis and external validity, there are three motivations for meta-analysis as an exercise in evidence accumulation.

First, meta-analysis can be used to *summarize* a set of estimates. When we have a set of related estimates, it is often useful to generate a numerical summary of them. In general, a meta-analysis summarizes estimates by reporting their (precision-weighted) average or properties of their distribution. When we have many estimates, such numeric summaries provide a form of quantitative synthesis of a literature. Critically, although such meta-analyses provide a quantitative summary, without much stronger theoretical commitments, that summary is not quantitatively related to anything deeper.

Second, some meta-analysis models impose a theoretical model of the cross-study environment that posits that observed estimates are "draws" from some underlying distribution. Under the assumption that the model is correct, the estimates obtained using meta-analysis can be used to *predict* the treatment effect in a yet-unrealized experiment. For example, the most commonly used meta-analysis estimator, the random-effects model, assumes that estimates are drawn from a normal distribution. The goal in these models is to estimate parameters of that normal distribution. If we have an estimate of the mean and variance of that distribution, we can, in principle, assess the likelihood that the next experiment will produce a treatment effect larger (or smaller) than some fixed value, x (assuming they are truly drawn from a normal distribution).

Third, by incorporating more than one estimate, meta-analyses incorporate additional information relative to constituent studies. Due to this pooling of estimates, meta-analytic estimates generally offer *precision gains* over the estimates from individual studies. See Slough et al. (2021) for an example applied to community monitoring of common-pool natural resources.

5.5 Application

We return to our running application – the pre-election information experiments in Brazil and Mexico – to illustrate our core points about meta-analysis. In the left column of Figure 3, we plot the intent-to-treat (ITT) estimates from Brazil and Mexico in the top panel.[23] Clearly, neither ITT is statistically distinguishable from zero: the point estimates are negative in both contexts,

---

[23] We estimate the ITT using OLS by estimating the following specification:

$$Y_{ib} = \beta_1 Z_i + g_b,$$

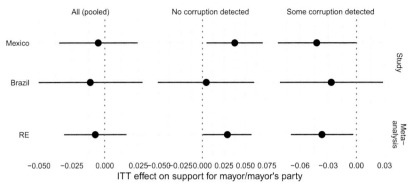

Figure 3 Meta-analytic estimates of the effect of audit result disclosure on vote choice for the incumbent (Brazil) or incumbent party (Mexico). The segments plot 95% confidence intervals.

but, both 95% confidence intervals overlap zero. The bottom panel plots the meta-analytic estimate of the common effect, as estimated by a random-effects model.

The important question with respect to whether this meta-analytic estimate has meaning, and thus a substantive interpretation, is whether there exists a common quantitative effect uniting the two studies. Theoretically, there are reasons to believe that it does not. The hypothesized mechanism, adverse selection, depends on both voters' prior beliefs and the content of information conveyed, not simply the presence versus absence of information. Recall that our treatment is simply defined as the presence or absence of the information (e.g., flyers) and that the content varies across the fliers as a function of the audit findings. Without this ancillary information, it is quite difficult to formulate a common effect. Moreover, design differences between the two studies could render the measurement of a common treatment effect untenable. One could argue that the outcome measure – a vote for the incumbent party in Mexico (where concurrent reelection is banned) – is distinct from a vote for the incumbent candidate in Brazil. For these measures to be harmonized, one would need to assert a correlation of 1 among members of the same party with respect to type or behavior, which is a distinct empirical question. When considering the

where Z_i is a treatment indicator (which varies at the individual level in Brazil and at the precinct level in Mexico) and g_b is a vector of block fixed effects (where blocks are groups of six to seven precincts in Mexico and municipalities in Brazil). β_1 is the estimator of the ITT. We cluster standard errors at the precinct level in Mexico and estimate heteroskedasticity-robust standard errors in Brazil. Note that in order to avoid post-treatment sample selection, we define Y_{ib} as an indicator for a vote for the incumbent/incumbent party, where $Y_i = 0$ corresponds to a vote for another party or abstention.

contrast, one could debate the presentation of corruption information. Perhaps most saliently, for the information treatment to produce the same effect, we need comparable levels of voter information among members of the control group in both sites. This is hard to assess empirically, even with common pre-treatment survey measures, since a level of information is ultimately about the relationship between beliefs about politician type/behavior and the actual politician's type/behavior. Importantly, these are not weaknesses of either study; rather, these issues emerge in the effort to combine the studies.

By inspection of Figure 3, the meta-analytic estimate in the left panel provides a quantitative summary of the two ITT estimates, and additionally offers precision gains (smaller confidence intervals) relative to both constituent studies. But neither of these benefits are meaningful if there is no quantitative connection between studies, since there would be no common underlying parameter to identify. Moreover, in order to use our parameter, and the statistical assumptions of the random-effects model, to predict the treatment in a third context, we must justify the existence, and quantitative generality, of this parameter.

Our meta-analysis of ITT effects in the left column of Figure 3 should likely be criticized on the basis of different signal content across municipalities within both studies. While Table 3 suggests that rates of the "clean" signals (no detected corruption in Mexico or accounts accepted in Brazil) administered in each study are comparable across contexts, but we are still "averaging" over two different effects of a mechanism. One response to this criticism of a lack of external validity is to calculate different subgroup ITTs by stratifying on signal content. This is precisely what we do in the center and right panels of Figure 3. This subgroup analysis follows the analytic strategy in Dunning et al. (2019a), but stratifies by signal content rather than some measure of the prior beliefs of voters relative to the signal. The center row corresponds to municipalities where no corruption was detected. The provision of information increases support for incumbent parties in Mexico ($p = 0.05$), while producing a smaller yet imprecisely estimated increase in support for incumbents in municipalities in Brazil. The estimated common effect in the lower panel is positive and significant ($p = 0.05$). In the right column, a signal of at least some corruption produces a negative effect in both contexts, which is statistically distinguishable from zero (at the $\alpha = 0.05$ level) in Mexico but not in Brazil. The meta-analytic estimate is negative and significant ($p = 0.03$). Note that this subgroup analysis is akin to meta-regression.[24] This stratification

---

[24] Random-effects meta-regression offers some regularization of estimates that is not present in the current stratification by subgroup.

may address some concerns about the lack of a common effect across settings. In other words, by separating out "good" from "bad" signals, there may be a better reason to believe that the same mechanisms will present in each setting, and may even produce the same effect in each setting – though these require theoretical justification.

The subgroup analysis does not, however, address the concerns about harmonization of the two experiments. In particular, the concerns about common outcome measures, and levels of voter information in the control condition, continue to present in the subgroup meta-analyses in Figure 3. In this way, the stratification of estimates on the basis of a theorized mechanism – adverse selection – is distinct from efforts or arguments that would need to be invoked to assuage concerns about the harmonization of the two studies.

Our discussion of the pre-electoral information experiments in Brazil and Mexico highlights two central concerns that should be addressed in any meta-analysis. Specifically, we need theoretical arguments to justify a quantitative relationship between studies that arise from a common mechanism, and thus give rise to a common effect. These concerns about mechanisms are needed to justify the assumption of external validity that, in part, justifies the existence of a common parameter that unites the studies. But exact external validity is not enough to guarantee identification of a common parameter. Meta-analysts also need to make sure that research designs are harmonized such that they "observe" the mechanism's effect in the same way. Our discussion of the Brazilian and Mexican experiments illustrate considerations that arguments for external validity and harmonization should invoke in any meta-analysis.

6 Replication

The second method for evidence accumulation we consider is *replication*, which *compares* the estimates from two or more constituent studies conducted on different samples or in different settings. One important goal of many replication projects is to draw an inference about a common mechanism by examining the relationship between measured estimates from different studies. While we discuss the replication of experiments, the concepts we discuss, and the results we motivate, apply to both experimental and observational work.[25]

Replication of an existing study in the social sciences can be approached one of two ways: *direct* or *conceptual* (Collins, 1992). Direct replication fixes three attributes of a study – the population (setting), contrast(s), and measurement strategies – and draws a new sample from the population using the same

---

[25] For a discussion on replication with observational studies, see Fariss and Jones (2018), Graham et al. (2023), and Fowler and Montagnes (2023).

sampling strategy. For example, if one conducted a survey experiment on a sample from an online panel, a direct replication would run the same survey experiment on a different sample from the same online panel, preserving the sampling strategy from the original experiment. Conceptual replications refer to replications where at least one of the three attributes – population (setting), contrast, or measurement strategy – is changed from the original experiment.

6.1 The Objective of Replication

What can be learned from replicating an existing study? Generally, there are four distinct motivations for conducting a replication exercise. Banerjee and Duflo (2009, p. 160) write: "To address . . . concerns about generalization, actual replication studies need to be carried out. Additional experiments have to be conducted in different locations, with different teams." Using a similar logic, Dunning (2016, p. S9) argues that "the only way to evaluate the external validity of an experimental result is to repeat the design in a new context." The first objective, then, is when replication is used to learn something about the external validity, or generalizability, of a mechanism using its measured effects. Consequently, replication is an empirical evaluation of whether similar findings are observed across contexts.

A related, second, motivation for replication projects is to measure the technology of intervention, through changes in treatments or measurement strategies. For example, Clayton et al. (2019) conduct a survey experiment to see whether the presence of women in political decision-making bodies changes citizen assessment of the legitimacy of the decisions made by these bodies. The main experimental manipulation varied the gender composition of the panel: The all-male treatment condition had eight males and zero females, whereas the gender-balanced condition had four males and four females. Respondents find anti-feminist decisions to be more legitimate when made by gender-balanced panel, rather than an all-male panel. In one replication experiment, they evaluate the degree to which this effect was driven by having a single ("token") woman by changing the treatment condition from a gender-balanced panel to a panel with only one woman. The replication probed the nature of the intervention, by seeing how the effect of interest changed in the contrast evaluated, thus seeing how changes in the instrument influenced the measured treatment effect. Indeed, they show a token female panel greatly attenuates the effect observed using a gender-balanced panel.

A third motivation for replication is to address concerns about statistical properties of studies. Specifically, every treatment effect is measured with some noise, which could mean that the observed estimate is larger or smaller than the target, instead resulting from an unusual draw. Replicating the experiment can assess the robustness of what was found in the original study. This motivation may be particularly salient when a study is underpowered, and thereby subject to greater variability. For example, Raffler et al. (2020) replicate an influential cluster-randomized study by Björkman and Svensson (2009) that contained only 50 clusters. The larger replication study contains 187 clusters.

A fourth motivation for replication is to identify and correct researcher error or pathologies of the publication process. Although some researcher error (or malfeasance) can be detected through the computational reproduction of code or the re-analysis of data, such efforts are distinct from replication. Instead, efforts to detect error and malfeasance through replication hinge on conducting new studies or gathering out-of-sample data. In psychology and economics, researchers have analyzed multiple replications simultaneously to learn about how easy it is to repeat the findings from a literature (Camerer et al., 2018; Open Science Collaboration, 2015). Comparison of measured effect sizes, test-statistics, or qualitative inferences can thus provide evidence about the replicability of a literature's most important findings.

6.2 Uniting Principles

The set of uniting principles invoked in a replication project depends critically on what the replication is being used to accomplish, that is, whether a replication project is geared toward learning about external validity, artifacts of a research design, or, instead, to examine statistical issues such as sample idiosyncrasies. Each goal corresponds to a different set of uniting principles.

6.2.1 External Validity or Artifacts of Design?

Some replication projects aim to assess the external validity of a mechanism. Other related efforts document various artifacts of a research design, to better understand the technologies of intervention that are used in different studies. In either case, accumulating evidence proceeds by making a comparison between two or more estimates to determine whether they provide consistent evidence about the same qualitative or quantitative relationship.

Determining whether a particular study constitutes a replication of another study largely revolves around a determination of whether the same mechanism is active in each of the respective settings. If the set Θ is the set of settings where a particular mechanism is active, then the *scope conditions* of the mechanism are represented by the boundary and properties of this set. Uniting Principle I is thus formulated (often implicitly) by these scope conditions. For example, if we were to take one candidate gender survey experiment and one candidate corruption study from the non-sensical meta-analysis in Chapter 4, and compare estimates, we would learn little from comparing the estimated treatment effects across the studies. This is because they lack a conceptual connection.

Rather, to sensibly compare estimates from two experiments providing information to voters, for example, a substantive argument ultimately must justify why constituent studies are united by a common mechanism. Here, Uniting Principle I is relatively straightforward. In particular, common concepts follows from *qualitative* statements about a mechanism and how it presents in multiple settings. This typically manifests through the inclusion criteria used to define what studies should be compared as part of a replication study.

The second uniting principle is about the quantitative relationship between constituent studies. It manifests more subtly in replication, depending on the goal. For some replication efforts, a quantitative equivalence is the desired goal. In such cases, the goal of the replication project is explicitly to measure the same finding in another place, or precisely measuring the part of the initially observed finding that should be expected to manifest elsewhere. In particular, if $\mathcal{E}_0$ is the original study, and $\mathcal{E}_r$ is its replication, the second uniting principle here requires target-equivalence between studies 0 and r, that is,

$$\tau_{m_0}^{\gamma_0}(\omega_0', \omega_0'' \mid \theta_0) = \tau_{m_r}^{\gamma_r}(\omega_r', \omega_r'' \mid \theta_r).$$

In other cases, however, scholars are not interested in replicating the exact same finding in another setting, but more modestly showing that the same qualitative relationship holds elsewhere. For instance, assessing whether an intervention improves an outcome when implemented, or whether it has no effect (or even a deleterious effect). Although such efforts may at first seem to be only about the conceptual relationship between studies, and therefore only invoke Uniting Principle I, this conclusion can be misleading as such efforts need a different, but important, quantitative relationship.

When the goal is to assess whether two empirical targets share the same sign, then target-equivalence is not the necessary criterion. Instead, one needs a criterion that is only sensitive to the sign of empirical targets.

TARGET-CONGRUENCE

Constituent studies, $\mathcal{E}_1 = \{m_1, (\omega_1', \omega_1''), \theta_1\}$ and $\mathcal{E}_2 = \{m_2, (\omega_2', \omega_2''), \theta_2\}$, are **target-congruent** if

$$sign\{\tau_{m_1}^{\gamma_1}(\omega_1', \omega_1'' \mid \theta_1)\} = sign\{\tau_{m_2}^{\gamma_2}(\omega_2', \omega_2'' \mid \theta_2)\}.$$

A meta-study has **target-congruence** if all constituent studies are target-congruent.

When interested in assessing the "directional" impact of a particular intervention, the relationship between empirical findings being compared assesses whether a contrast produces a positive (i.e., >0), as opposed to nonpositive (i.e., ≤ 0), empirical target. Such an assessment only makes sense when the meaning of 0 is the same across empirical targets, that is, it requires that between studies 0 and r,

$$sign\{\tau^{\gamma}_{m_0}(\omega'_0, \omega''_0 \mid \theta_0)\} = sign\{\tau^{\gamma}_{m_r}(\omega'_r, \omega''_r \mid \theta_r)\}.$$

This condition requires that empirical targets cross 0 in the same places, that is,

$$\tau^{\gamma_0}_{m_0}(\omega'_0, \omega''_0 \mid \theta_0) = 0 \quad \Leftrightarrow \quad \tau^{\gamma_r}_{m_r}(\omega'_r, \omega''_r \mid \theta_r) = 0,$$

and at these points (where they are both zero)

$$\nabla \tau^{\gamma_0}_{m_0}(\omega'_0, \omega''_0 \mid \theta_0) \geq (<) \, 0 \quad \Leftrightarrow \quad \nabla \tau^{\gamma_r}_{m_r}(\omega'_r, \omega''_r \mid \theta_r) \geq (<) \, 0,$$

where ∇ refers to the gradient operator. Thus, target-congruence is logically weaker than target-equivalence because it places fewer restrictions on how empirical targets must match. They can differ almost everywhere as long as their sign remains consistent across settings.

6.2.2 Assessing Statistical Issues

In order to assess the magnitude, or direction, of statistical discrepancies between empirical findings, constituent studies need to aim at the same target. This requires invocation of both qualitative and quantitative uniting principles. Like the other goals of replication already discussed, researchers must assume that a common mechanism arises in each setting. We would not expect to learn about the statistical properties of an estimate of the effect of corruption information provision on pro-incumbent voting from an experiment on voting for women candidates. But this qualitative uniting principle is too weak to learn about statistical discrepancies between estimates.

In order to isolate the difference in statistical noise between two estimates, both estimates need to shoot at the same target, and thus satisfy target-equivalence. To see why, consider the estimates of treatment effects obtained from two studies, e_1 and e_2, as they relate to their respective empirical targets:

$$e_1 = \overbrace{\tau^{\gamma_1}_{m_1}(\omega'_1, \omega''_1 \mid \theta_1)}^{\text{Empirical target}} + \overbrace{\varepsilon_1}^{\text{Noise}}$$
$$e_2 = \tau^{\gamma_2}_{m_2}(\omega'_2, \omega''_2 \mid \theta_2) + \varepsilon_2.$$

Empirical targets measure the influence of a mechanism under a specific comparison and measurement strategy, but the target and noise terms in each estimate have different properties. Under the typical assumption that potential outcomes are fixed, this quantity is necessarily *non-random*. In contrast, the noise terms, ε_1 and ε_2 are random and, for most estimators, follow a known asymptotic distribution. When comparing e_1 and e_2 to assess the likelihood of observing differences of a particular size, differences between the non-random targets need to be eliminated.[26] Thus, in order to make inferences about the noise terms, one must assume a deterministic quantitative relationship between targets, as well as distributional assumptions about the noise terms.

6.3 Hypothesis Tests

Replication projects are fundamentally exercises in comparing the estimates from different studies. Consequently, they require some criteria to evaluate a comparison. To this end, we discuss two frequent hypothesis tests that are used in replication projects. While both tests fulfill the first uniting principle in the same way, they differ in how they fulfill Uniting Principle II.

Replication can be used to assess empirically the presence (or absence) of external validity. In particular, replication can be used to assess the two specific forms of cross-sectional external validity we detailed in Chapter 3. We now consider the hypothesis tests associated with each form of external validity. We first consider **estimate-comparison tests**, which evaluate a null hypothesis that two or more empirical targets are quantitatively equivalent.

ESTIMATE-COMPARISON TEST

The **estimate-comparison test** computes:

$$Z(e_1, e_2) = e_1 - e_2$$

and test the null hypothesis

$$H_0: \tau_{m_1}^{\gamma}(\omega_1', \omega_1'' | \theta_1) = \tau_{m_2}^{\gamma}(\omega_2', \omega_2'' | \theta_2)$$

against the alternative

$$H_a: \tau_{m_1}^{\gamma}(\omega_1', \omega_1'' | \theta_1) \neq \tau_{m_2}^{\gamma}(\omega_2', \omega_2'' | \theta_2).$$

---

[26] One could alternatively assume a specific relationship between targets, for example, the constant $d \neq 0$ given by $d = \tau_{m_1}^{\gamma}(\omega_1', \omega_1'' | \theta_1) - \tau_{m_2}^{\gamma}(\omega_2', \omega_2'' | \theta_2)$. This corresponds to a relabeling of empirical targets, and it seems easier to ensure that $d = 0$ than to know d.

While the estimate-comparison test evaluates the equivalence between *estimates*, it is used to make an inference about the equivalence of the empirical targets that produce those estimates. Importantly, estimates, if different, could be different for at least three reasons:

1. The mechanisms across studies lack exact external validity so that the empirical targets are different even when research designs are harmonized;
2. Variation in the research design across studies, which means that the constituent studies (artifactually) aim at different targets;
3. Idiosyncracies in samples, realized treatment assignments, or measurement error produce statistical noise.

Without a more elaborate model of the cross-study environment, the estimate-comparison test does not permit inferences about why empirical targets are different (if, for instance, the null hypothesis has been rejected). Moreover, a failure to reject the null hypothesis cannot be interpreted as evidence of exact external validity without further assumptions. In the next section, we discuss the assumptions that are necessary to move from an inference about the equivalence of empirical targets to an inference about external validity or artifactual differences between studies.

Simple modifications allow for different estimate-comparison tests, depending on the quantitative relationship between empirical targets. As an example, if the empirical target in setting 1 is expected to be twice the target in setting 2, for every measurement strategy and contrast, then this could be reflected in the test-statistic, Z. Specifically, the estimate-comparison test would instead use the test-statistic $Z(e_1, e_2) = 2e_1 - e_2$, to test for quantitative equivalence, according the posited quantitative relationship.

The second hypothesis test that we examine is one that is frequently used in replication projects and relies on a comparison of the *sign* of estimates. Such tests are used to make an inference about the congruence between the *signs* of the empirical targets across constituent studies. We refer to targets that share the same sign as being *sign-congruent* and tests of this property as **sign-comparison tests**. Such tests evaluate a null hypothesis that the empirical targets share the same sign (e.g., positive, negative, or zero), which is (logically) less stringent than the null hypothesis of the estimate-comparison test. By less stringent, we mean that the null hypothesis of the estimate-comparison test (that the targets are equivalent) implies the null hypothesis of the sign-comparison test (that the targets are sign-congruent). However, the null hypothesis of the sign-comparison test does not imply the null hypothesis of the estimate-comparison test.

Sign-Comparison Test

The **sign-comparison test** computes:

$$Z(e_1, e_2) = e_1 \cdot e_2$$

and tests the null hypothesis

$$H_0: sign\{\tau_{m_1}^{\gamma}(\omega_1', \omega_1''|\theta_1)\} = sign\{\tau_{m_2}^{\gamma}(\omega_2', \omega_2''|\theta_2)\}$$

against the alternative

$$H_a: sign\{\tau_{m_1}^{\gamma}(\omega_1', \omega_1''|\theta_1)\} \neq sign\{\tau_{m_2}^{\gamma}(\omega_2', \omega_2''|\theta_2)\}.$$

The sign-comparison test is often conducted heuristically. This means that researchers simply compare the signs (or significance) of estimates rhetorically but do not calculate a *p*-value or conduct inference. This approach can be particularly misleading when one estimate is, for example, positive and significant (for some Type-I error rate, α), while the other is positive but not significant. Comparison of signs is frequent in literature reviews or review articles through statements of the form "Author A finds evidence that a related treatment increases outcome *Y*. We, however, do not detect evidence that treatment changes *Y*." While this approach may be sufficient in a non-technical review of the literature, if the goal is to explicitly compare estimates in studies 1 and 2, such an approach can lead to exceptionally high type-I error rates (false rejections of the null hypothesis of sign-congruence). Another reason for the use of heuristic sign-comparison tests is presumably that this test is not standard in most statistical software packages.

Brinch et al. (2017) provide a straightforward method for inference on the sign-comparison test given two estimates e_1 and e_2 and their respective standard errors se_1 and se_2.[27] To do so, construct *T*-statistics, $T_j = \frac{e_j}{se_j}$, for both estimates, and compute the following:

1. Test the null hypothesis that $\{e_1 < 0\} \cap \{e_2 < 0\}$ by calculating one-sided (lower) *p*-values for both T_1 and T_2, denoted $\underline{p}_1$ and $\underline{p}_2$, respectively. Implement a Bonferroni correction, denoted by $B(\cdot)$. Select the minimum Bonferroni-corrected *p*-value, $\underline{p} = \min\{B(\underline{p}_1), B(\underline{p}_2)\}$.
2. Test the null hypothesis that $\{e_1 > 0\} \cap \{e_2 > 0\}$ by calculating one-sided (upper) *p*-values for both T_1 and T_2, denoted $\bar{p}_1$ and $\bar{p}_2$, respectively. As in Step #1, implement a Bonferroni correction and select the minimum Bonferroni-corrected *p*-value, $\bar{p} = \min\{B(\bar{p}_1), B(\bar{p}_2)\}$.

---

[27] See Brinch et al. (2017) Appendix B. and Slough and Tyson (2024) Appendix D.

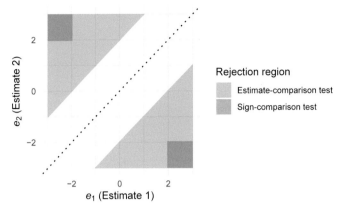

Figure 4 Rejection regions for the estimate-comparison and sign-comparison test, $\alpha = 0.05$. We assume that the standard errors of both estimates are 1 in order to visualize these regions in two dimensions.

3. The sign-comparison test tests the null hypothesis that (e_1, e_2) is an element of the union of the two convex subsets described in steps #1 and #2. Following Berger (1982), the *p*-value for this test is given by $p = \max\{\underline{p}, \overline{p}\}$.

Note that because the null hypothesis of the sign-comparison test is less stringent (or weaker) than the estimate-comparison test, it is *harder* to reject the null hypothesis that the targets share the same sign than the null hypothesis that the targets are equivalent. We show this pattern in Figure 4 by overlaying the rejection regions of the two tests for a Type-I error rate of $\alpha = 0.05$. The rejection regions of the sign-comparison test are contained within the rejection regions of the estimate-comparison test. This is precisely the opposite conclusion of what emerges from many heuristic sign-comparison tests, which shows why this practice leads to incorrect inferences about sign-congruence.

As in our discussion of the estimate-comparison test, inferences from the sign-comparison test do not tell us why targets have a different sign or why we cannot reject this null hypothesis. Further assumptions are necessary to yield these important substantive inferences about external validity or study artifacts. To this point, our discussion has centered on tests that can be conducted with a single study and its replication. These baseline tests form the basis for the analyses pursued in larger replication studies. When there are two or more replications of a given experiment, researchers can make multiple pairwise comparisons of studies or test a joint null hypothesis of target-equivalence or target-congruence. As the number of replications increases, researchers have more "data" (estimates). However, as we will discuss, this may complicate the process of learning about external validity or study artifacts. Alternatively, inspired by many meta-scientific efforts to address the replicability of a literature or field (e.g., Camerer et al., 2018; Open Science Collaboration, 2015), researchers typically make comparisons within each set of replications. With multiple distinct replications, it is possible to summarize features of the distribution of estimates or test-statistics across replications, for example, by reporting the distribution of differences in estimates. This exercise can provide evidence consistent with publication bias in a literature.

6.4 Assessing External Validity or Harmonization

One strength of replication over meta-analysis or extrapolation-based approaches is that replication does not necessarily presume external validity. Consequently, it can be used to test for evidence of external validity (or lack thereof). Yet, as we have discussed, additional assumptions are required to learn about external validity under either the estimate- or sign-comparison tests.

The challenge in devising statistical tests for external validity is to align the null hypotheses of these tests with relevant concepts of external validity. Focusing on the estimate-comparison test, recall that it evaluates a null hypothesis of target-equivalence. We know from our discussion of Slough and Tyson (2023) that exact external validity (as defined in Chapter 3) and harmonization are necessary and sufficient to ensure target-equivalence. This result implies that if research designs are harmonized between a study and its replication, then the null hypothesis of target-equivalence becomes a null hypothesis of exact external validity. In other words, harmonization of constituent studies ensures that estimate-comparison tests permit evaluation of exact external validity.

By a similar logic, suppose that a mechanism's exact external validity holds across two studies, perhaps because the studies were conducted in the same setting, or because of a broadly accepted theoretical argument. If this were the case, the null hypothesis of target-equivalence instead becomes a null hypothesis of design harmonization, allowing for an empirical test of harmonization.

Our analysis suggests that the estimate-comparison test can evaluate exact external validity or harmonization, but not both. Specifically, both exact external validity and harmonization cannot be assessed simultaneously – one must be established independently or assumed to test for the other. Otherwise, failures of target-equivalence cannot be attributed to a failure of either exact external validity or harmonization. The quantitative relationship between empirical targets can only vary along one dimension in order to definitively test for quantitative equivalence on that dimension.

The sign-comparison test follows a similar logic. The null hypothesis of target-congruence corresponds to a weaker notion: sign-congruent external validity, as introduced in Chapter 3. (Slough and Tyson, 2024, Theorem 1) prove that harmonization and sign-congruent external validity are necessary and sufficient for target-congruence. As a result, under harmonization of study designs, the null hypothesis of target-congruence is equivalent to a null hypothesis of sign-congruent external validity. Thus, the sign-comparison test allows for assessment of sign-congruent external validity, but only when the constituent studies are harmonized.

The sign-comparison test does not provide an analogous test for harmonization, however. Sign-congruent external validity does not allow us to "pin down" the possible set of treatment effects sufficiently to make target-congruence equivalent to harmonization. As such, the sign-comparison test can test for (one concept of) external validity, but it does not offer a test for harmonization. We summarize this discussion in Table 4 for clear reference. The estimate-comparison test employs a null hypothesis of target-equivalence and the sign-comparison test employs a null hypothesis of target-congruence. One potential limitation of these null hypotheses is that an underpowered replication will be unlikely to reject the relevant null hypothesis.[28] We suggest these null hypotheses because they align with a view of replication as a potentially

Table 4 When can the estimate-comparison or sign-comparison test permit inferences about external validity or harmonization?

Test	Assumption	Interpretation of null hypothesis	Tests for
Estimate-comparison	Harmonization	A null hypothesis of target-equivalence becomes one of *exact external validity*	Exact external validity
Estimate-comparison	Exact external validity	A null hypothesis of target-equivalence becomes one of *harmonization*	Harmonization
Sign-comparison	Harmonization	A null hypothesis target-congruence becomes one of *sign-congruent external validity*	Sign-congruent external validity

---

[28] When replicating an underpowered study, even a highly powered replication faces similar issues.

adversarial endeavor. They put the burden on an independent or adversarial replicator to find evidence that is *inconsistent* with target-equivalence or target-congruence. This should promote the use of highly powered replication designs. In a non-adversarial context, however, researchers might be tempted to employ an underpowered replication in order to reduce the likelihood that they find evidence against target-equivalence/target-congruence. In such a setting, equivalence tests present one principled way to incentivize replicators to adopt high-powered replication designs. It is straightforward to formulate an equivalence test analogous to the estimate-comparison test following Hartman and Hidalgo (2018). For the analogue to the sign-comparison test, one can specify a null hypothesis of $sign\{\tau_{m_1}^{\gamma}(\omega_1', \omega_1''|\theta_1)\} \neq sign\{\tau_{m_2}^{\gamma}(\omega_2', \omega_2''|\theta_2)\}$ and modify the above procedure for inference accordingly.

Much of our discussion of replication has focused on two studies (or a study and its replication) but applies to more than two studies measuring the influence of a common mechanism. The addition of more studies can make inferences about external validity or artifactual discrepancies more difficult. For example, if we are trying to learn whether a mechanism has external validity, all constituent studies must be harmonized. Increasing the number of studies increases the possibility of failures of harmonization, which can undermine inferences about external validity. This is not a statistical problem: if studies lack harmonization, they are apt to aim at different empirical targets. As such, the conventional logic for statistical concerns – more data (e.g., more studies) are better than less data (e.g., fewer studies) – does not hold. In this case, adding more non-harmonized studies stymies efforts to learn about external validity of a mechanism because determining whether observed differences in effects are due to harmonization failures or a lack of external validity is impossible. This feature is established formally in Slough and Tyson (2024, Theorem 2).

6.5 Application

We return to our discussion of the information experiments in Brazil and Mexico in order to highlight the concepts that we develop in our discussion of replication. We first implement the estimate- and sign-comparison tests in Table 5. The ITT estimates reported are those that are plotted in Figure 3. We see that we are unable to reject any of the null hypotheses that we test for in any of the three samples we discussed. Does the failure to reject the null hypothesis allow us to make a substantive inference about the external validity of these effects? Does it provide information about harmonization? Drawing inferences about external validity or sign-congruent external validity from estimate- or sign-comparison tests requires that we consider the possibility of other sources of discrepancy in the estimates. First, we need the estimators of

Table 5 ITT estimates/p-values from the estimate- and sign-comparison tests

| Sample | ITT estimates with 95% CIs | | p-values from | |
	Brazil	Mexico	Estimate-comparison	Sign-comparison
All	−0.011 [−0.050, 0.028]	−0.002 [−0.037, 0.033]	0.738	1.00
Good signal	0.004 [−0.051, 0.060]	0.037 [0.0005, 0.070]	0.318	1.00
Bad signal	−0.027 [−0.082, 0.028]	−0.042 [−0.084, −0.001]	0.659	1.00

treatment effects to be unbiased and consistent. This is fairly straightforward in the above example. Both are well-designed and well-executed experiments. At the very least, there exists no evidence of manipulation or poor administration that would lead to concerns of bias.

When inferences about external validity or sign-congruent external validity are sought, however, we further need to ensure that the research designs are harmonized. We discussed some of the threats to harmonization in our discussion of meta-analysis, so this discussion should be familiar. First, the outcome of a vote for the incumbent party in Mexico versus a vote for the incumbent (candidate) in Brazil is due to differences in term limits and the purposeful selection of first-term mayors in Brazil. Second, assessment of status-quo levels of voter information, and hence the possible space for voter learning across contexts. This speaks to the potential for a lack of contrast harmonization.

If we are satisfied with arguments or evidence of harmonization, the tests in Table 5 can be interpreted as a failure to reject a null hypothesis of external validity (estimate-comparison test) or sign-congruent external validity (sign-comparison test). It is important to note how these tests compare to current practice. In current practice, many scholars would assert a lack of (sign-congruent) external validity in the "good signal" condition because we reject the null hypothesis in Mexico but fail to do so in Brazil. Similarly, in the "bad signal" condition, we reject the null hypothesis in Mexico but not Brazil. Assessing (separately) null hypotheses that treatment effects are equal to zero does not constitute a test of any form of external validity because the null hypotheses do not posit anything about the *relationship* between the targets of the studies, whereas the sign-comparison test does.

Suppose, instead, that we were interested in assessing the degree to which different artifacts in the design of these studies change voter responses to information. This is an important test if, for example, we were seeking to design the "optimal" informational flier. To use these tests to interpret whether there exist artifacts in the design that (significantly) change treatment effects, we would assume external validity across the Mexican and Brazilian studies. As we already discussed, an argument for external validity is most likely to be satisfied in the good and bad signal conditions. Here, we would rely exclusively on the estimate-comparison test. We do not detect evidence that the bundle of design artifacts – here, different outcome measurement, potentially different levels of information in control, and different presentation of the information on fliers – affect the measured treatment effects.

There are limits to testing the influence of design artifacts on treatment effects. First, we may be interested in attributes of the intervention that can be manipulated, namely, the content of the fliers. This test cannot isolate a specific difference between the studies when the studies vary on multiple dimensions. Indeed, it is possible that differences in flier content are counterbalanced by differences in baseline voter information. This is not detectable without additional treatment arms or other purposeful variation in the attributes of the design. Second, this test rests on the assumption of exact external validity. Much of the literature we discuss has emerged because of doubts about the plausibility of a mechanism's external validity.

Finally, what must we assume to interpret the tests in Table 5 as tests for researcher error or integrity? We first emphasize that we do not have any basis for concern about the studies that we discuss on this dimension. Indeed, as Metaketa studies, these studies have been subject to an unusually high level of scrutiny and volume of replication/reuse. These forms of computational reproduction are distinct from replication, but also serve to assuage some potential concerns with regard to researcher error or integrity. Our point in this section is that in order to use the Brazil study to assess the integrity or veracity of the Mexico study (or vice versa), we would need to establish independently (or assume) both exact external validity and harmonization. Only then can the estimate-comparison test can be interpreted as a test for issues of research integrity.

Our discussion of replication as a tool to improve research integrity is important because it emphasizes that we should design replications differently if the goal is to assess statistical issues (or the behavior that belies these issues) than if the goal is to assess external validity (or design artifacts). In other words, to test for external validity it is necessary to fix (harmonize) the study design but vary the setting. But varying the setting limits our ability to assess statistical issues because it requires an assumption of exact external validity. Clarifying the goals of replication can help us to assess the congruence between replication study design and the inferences they support.

7 Extrapolation

Extrapolation is an increasingly popular approach to the generalization of results from a single study devoted to studying a particular phenomenon. We discuss it in this Element for two reasons. First, many recent developments in statistics, economics, and political methodology have focused on extrapolation-based approaches to assessing the generality of empirical findings, and thus external validity. Second, extrapolation approaches are often advocated as a way to learn about external validity when it is not possible to conduct or identify another study that measures the influence of a mechanism. Evidence accumulation and extrapolation are different in that evidence accumulation constitutes an empirical approach to studying external validity, whereas extrapolation is a theoretical model-based approach. In this section, using uniting principles, we discuss what can be learned about the external validity of mechanisms from extrapolation-based approaches.

Current approaches to extrapolation rely on a special class of structural models that are used to extrapolate (or transport) estimates from a realized study to different settings or theoretical populations. We show that, as an inferential strategy, extrapolation approaches are analogous to selection-on-observables in the single-study setting, and thus constitute a significant departure from the principles of the credibility revolution, as articulated in Chapter 1 (with the exception of Gechter and Meager (2021)). We highlight a tension that emerges between the invocation of design-based arguments for within-study identification of causal effects and the reliance on structural or model-based extrapolation approaches for causal generalization.

7.1 The Objective of Extrapolation

Extrapolation-based approaches to transporting estimates from an observed sample to an unobserved population, or from an observed context to an unobserved context, aim to estimate what the treatment effect *would* be in the unobserved setting. This estimate can serve multiple purposes.

First, suppose one audience for impact evaluation is a policymaker. The policymaker seeks to use the results of an experiment to determine whether to conduct the intervention in their jurisdiction. However, the experiment only studies the intervention within a subset of individuals or communities, or from a different jurisdiction altogether. In either case, the policymaker must speculate about how results translate from the sample on which the study's results are based to the population on which they want the policy to apply, or from the jurisdiction in which the study was conducted to the policymaker's jurisdiction. Methods for extrapolation of treatment effects mirror the policymaker's considerations.

Second, researchers may seek to answer the question "how different would (average) treatment effects be in a different setting?" This may be a matter of curiosity or a response to broader concerns about the generalization of empirical findings. In the absence of a study or experiment in the unobserved setting, extrapolation provides one quantitative response to this question.[29] Some researchers seek to go further by quantifying the difference between the observed estimate and the extrapolated estimate. For example, Egami and Hartman (2023) term the difference between a sample treatment effect and a grand population treatment effect "external validity bias," and Findley et al. (2021) pursue a similar decomposition strategy to explore possible differences between the sample treatment effect and the population treatment effect.

7.2 Uniting Principles

As in the case of meta-studies and evidence accumulation, extrapolation approaches also invoke uniting principles, and it is these uniting principles that bestow a substantive – and potentially causal – interpretation to the output of an extrapolation exercise. Specifically, it is the uniting principles that underlie the claim that a causal effect measured in one setting, where an intervention was conducted, can be used to impute a causal effect somewhere else.

Extrapolation approaches tend to use uniting principles differently than replications and meta-analyses. In the latter, uniting principles formulate how the evidence collected in multiple settings can be combined or compared explicitly. Extrapolation, on the other hand, uses uniting principles to link settings where empirical findings were observed with settings where they were not. Thus, the uniting principles used in an extrapolation exercise serve a speculative – rather than an evaluative – purpose.

Similar to the cases of meta-analysis and replication discussed above, any extrapolation exercise fulfills both uniting principles. In particular, when extrapolating from one setting to another, a qualitative conceptual connection between settings is presumed, a feature which is widely appreciated. For instance, few scholars would assert that an experiment on candidate gender and vote choice could be used to impute the effects of a corruption-revealing intervention in a different setting or population. Approaches that heavily rely on the grand-sampling formulation of the cross-study environment and aim to impute a population average treatment effect, assume that the imputed effect corresponds to some unadulterated influence of the mechanism of interest which manifests in the (grand) population.

---

[29] One alternative to extrapolation is to use a theory or argument to postulate (qualitatively) why and how effects may be similar (or not) in a different setting.

Uniting Principle II must also be fulfilled in any extrapolation exercise, thereby necessitating specification of a quantitative relationship. Because extrapolation approaches tend to focus on imputing a speculative finding from an empirical finding, the quantitative relationship between source and destination is crucial. Consequently, fulfilling Uniting Principle II typically invokes a model of the cross-study environment which specifies an invertible mapping between a source and each destination. Importantly, these projections are not testable features of the cross-study environment absent some experiment in the unobserved setting. Most models of the cross-study environment fulfill Uniting Principle II, and in so doing formulate ontological positions on the source (e.g., its existence), and the mechanism's external validity across destinations. The specific form of the models vary by approach, as we detail in the following section.

7.3 External Validity and Extrapolation

Most approaches to extrapolation are consistent with some form of projective external validity, where the empirical target of the study under consideration is a destination that has been projected on from some source. More specifically, the observed result, such as the sample average treatment effect (SATE), has come from some other object, like a population level average treatment effect (PATE). Presupposing the relationship that connects a source to destinations ($\pi(\cdot)$ from Chapter 3) necessarily invokes a projective formulation of external validity. However, omission of an explicit discussion of this feature muddles the relationship between extrapolation methods and (some concept of) external validity. Specifically, these methods *assume* a projective concept of external validity. To illustrate the link between standard assumptions and our projective concept of external validity, we highlight two examples.

We first consider an example that invokes external validity to estimate the PATE from the SATE: Egami and Hartman (2023). We alter their notation to maintain consistency with the rest of this Element.

EXAMPLE 1

Suppose there is some population of units, $\mathcal{U}$. Let $X_u \in \mathbb{R}^k$ for some integer $k < +\infty$ be some set of covariates for unit $u \in \mathcal{U}$, and let S_u be an indicator denoting whether unit $u \in \mathcal{U}$ has been sampled ($S_u = 1$) or not ($S_u = 0$). For a fixed measurement strategy, m, and contrast (ω', ω''), Egami and Hartman (2023, p. 5) define

Definition 1 *Ignorability of Sampling and Treatment Effect Heterogeneity*

$$Y_u^m(\omega'' \mid S_u) - Y_u^m(\omega' \mid S_u)$$

is independent of sample status, S_u, after conditioning on covariates, X_u.

Definition 1 holds that, conditional on pre-treatment covariates, X_u, all unit-specific individual treatment effects, $Y_u^m(\omega'') - Y_u^m(\omega')$, are independent of sampling into the experiment. From the perspective of external validity, this expression holds that potential outcomes – and, by extension, individual treatment effects – do not depend on the sampling status of a unit. This, then, implies that the same mechanism(s) would be activated for any unit whether a treatment was administered to the sample or to the population. In particular, this rules out any kind of intervention whose effect depends on its scale. Instead, if effects depend on the scale of the intervention, the scale determines what profile of mechanisms is activated, in which case potential outcomes depend on measured features of the sample, X_u.

What matters for us is that the kind of formulation of the cross-study environment put forward in Example 1, and in particular, that unit-level potential outcomes, and hence treatment effects, are independent of sampling status, imposes a specific formulation of external validity, namely, that X_u is a sufficient statistic for setting. For the purposes of extrapolation, assuming such a form of external validity is needed to construct a mapping from the source (the population) to the destination (the sample).

Our second example comes from Pearl and Bareinboim (2011, 2014).

Example 2

Suppose there is an outcome of interest, Y, a treatment, ω, and a covariate X. In setting 1, the distribution $P_1(Y, \omega, X)$ is different from that in setting 2, $P_2(Y, \omega, X)$, via the transport formula:

$$P_2(Y(\omega) \mid X(\omega)) = \int_z P_1(Y(\omega) \mid X(\omega)) P_2(z), \qquad (10)$$

which says that the probability of potential outcome $Y(\omega)$ in setting 2 is the reweighted average, according to X, of the probability of having potential outcome $Y(\omega)$ in setting 1.

Pearl and Bareinboim (2014, p. 588) write:

> *S*-variables [selection variables] locate the mechanisms where structural discrepancies between the two populations are suspected to take place. Alternatively, the absence of a selection node pointing to a variable represents the assumption that the mechanism responsible for assigning value to that variable is the same in the two populations. In the extreme case, we could add selection nodes to all variables, which means that we have no reason to believe that the populations share any mechanism in common, and this, of course would inhibit any exchange of information among the populations. The invariance assumptions between populations, as we will see, will open the door for the transport of some experimental findings.

The transportability approach of Pearl and Bareinboim (2011, 2014) assumes that treatment effects are produced by multiple mechanisms. The quote above, and equation (10), make clear that the transport formula *assumes* a structure on the set of mechanisms, which may or may not be true across contexts.

The transport formula is predicated on the idea that no mechanism is observed in isolation, that is, there are always other mechanisms that are present and some of them *must* be common across settings. Consequently, the transport formula, (10), seemingly applies to a wider class of relationships between experimental settings because they require fewer invariance assumptions (relative to Example #1). However, this can be misleading since the transport formula assumes design invariance. In particular, if there is only one mechanism, then the transport formula reduces to the identity function, that is, equation (10) reduces to

$$P_2(Y(\omega) \mid X(\omega)) = \int_z P_1(Y(\omega) \mid X(\omega))P_2(z) = P_1(Y(\omega) \mid X(\omega)).$$

This illustrates just what the transportability approach of Pearl and Bareinboim (2011, 2014) assumes about the cross-study environment – a mechanism has a uniform influence in every setting. What leads to heterogeneity is the presence of *other mechanisms*. This matters because it assumes the external validity of the mechanism of interest, and models the heterogeneity of the observed treatment effect as coming from other mechanism(s), rather than failures of exact external validity (which are ruled out by construction).

7.4 Extrapolation and the Credibility Revolution

Prior to the credibility revolution, quantitative empirical social science was heavily model-based, and the most common method of identifying quantitative measures of causal effects was *selection-on-observables*. One of the motivations of the wide-scale adoption of design-based strategies for causal inference is the acknowledgment that the fidelity of model-based approaches lacked a clear substantive motivation (e.g., Leamer, 1983). The primary concern was to reduce the threat of bias due to unobserved confounding factors, which can induce bias with unknown magnitude and direction. The credibility revolution advanced and developed various models of research design and estimators to address this concern and better measure unbiased estimates of (specific) causal effects.

Existing approaches and methods of extrapolation are all variants of selection-on-observables. In particular, both the grand sampling and transportability approaches require specification of observed variables that predict activation of a mechanism. In grand sampling (or X-validity) approaches, individual-level covariates must predict treatment variation in conditional average treatment effects and these covariates must be observed by the analyst. In transportability approaches, context-level observable variables need to predict variation in mechanism activation, and again, these covariates need to be observed by the analyst. Given the wide-scale reluctance to rely on model-based methods at the level of a constituent study, it is unclear why such models should be trusted to account for things like treatment effect heterogeneity but not selection into treatment. Specifically, the return to selection-on-observables to characterize the cross-study environment reintroduces familiar issues from the single-study setting. We present a simple example to illustrate how extrapolation-based approaches fall prey to the same issues – here, omitted variable bias – that plague more pedestrian research designs.

Consider conducting an experiment to measure a sample average treatment effect (SATE), with the goal of estimating the population average treatment effect (PATE). Suppose that units in both the population and the sample can be characterized by two binary covariates: $X_1 \in \{0, 1\}$ and $X_2 \in \{0, 1\}$. In the sample, $\Pr(X_1 = 1) = \frac{1}{2}$ and $\Pr(X_2 = 1) = \frac{1}{2}$, but X_1 and X_2 are correlated according to $\rho \in (-1, 1)$. Common support assumptions with respect to sampling are satisfied: units in all cells enter the sample $S_u = 1$ with probability $0 < \Pr(S_u = 1) < 1$. We report the joint and marginal distributions of X_1 and X_2 in the sample and population in Table 6. It should be clear from inspection of the marginal distributions of X_1 and X_2 that – as is standard in practice – the sample is not a (simple) random sample of the population.

Suppose only X_1 is measured prior to the experiment, perhaps because X_2's importance was not known or because X_2 was not readily measurable. Unfortunately, all causal heterogeneity, and thus treatment effects, are predicted by X_2. Individual treatment effects are given by

$$ITE_u = X_{2u} + 0.2(1 - X_{2u}),$$

Table 6　Joint and marginal distributions of X_1 and X_2

Sample

		X_2		
		0	1	
X_1	0	$0.25(1 + \rho)$	$0.25(1 - \rho)$	0.5
	1	$0.25(1 - \rho)$	$0.25(1 + \rho)$	0.5
		0.5	0.5	

Population

		X_2		
		0	1	
X_1	0	0.25	0.4	0.65
	1	0.15	0.2	0.35
		0.4	0.6	

which implies that an ITE_u is 0.2 when $X_{2u} = 0$ and 1 when $X_{2u} = 1$. Treatment effects do not vary in X_{1u}, the measured covariate. This formulation of ITEs is important for extrapolation. Specifically, it says that treatment effects do not depend on whether a unit is sampled or not, and reflects Definition 1 above.[30] Using the marginal distribution of X_2 in the lower panel of Table 6, it is straightforward to see that the PATE is

$$PATE = 0.4 \times 0.2 + 0.6 \times 1 = 0.68.$$

Moreover, the (true) SATE is

$$SATE = 0.5 \times 0.2 + 0.5 \times 1 = 0.6,$$

which does not depend on the correlation between X_1 and X_2 because treatment effects do not depend on X_1.

Suppose researchers were to use X_1, the only observed covariate to extrapolate the PATE from the observed SATE.[31] To estimate the PATE, denote by $\psi_x = \Pr(X_1 = x)$ in the theoretical population, and since the treatment is indexed

---

[30]　Egami and Hartman (2023, p. 4) formalize this assumption as $Y_u(T = 1, c) - Y_u(T = 0, c) \perp S_u | \mathbf{X}_u$, where T is a treatment indicator, c is the context (or setting) where the study was conducted, S_u is an indicator for whether a unit is in the sample, and $\mathbf{X}_u$ is a matrix of covariates.

[31]　There exist several estimators used for extrapolation. Egami and Hartman (2023) classify these estimators as weights-based, outcome-based, and doubly robust. In this simple example with a single binary covariate, all estimators produce indistinguishable estimates $\widehat{PATE}$.

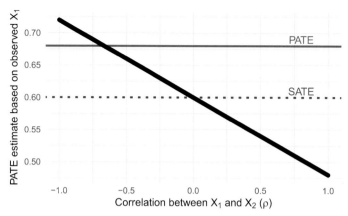

Figure 5 Estimates of *PATE* between observed X_1 and unobserved X_2 (see Table 6). The plot shows that omission of X_2 biases estimates of the PATE.

by $\omega_u \in \{0, 1\}$ and $S_u = 1$ indicates that a unit is in the experimental sample, we have that

$$\widehat{PATE}$$

$$= \sum_{x \in X_1} \underbrace{\psi_x}_{\substack{\text{Population} \\ \text{proportion}}} \underbrace{\left[\widehat{E}[Y_u | \omega_u = 1, X_1 = x, S_u = 1] - \widehat{E}[Y_u | \omega_u = 0, X_1 = x, S_u = 1] \right]}_{\text{Sample CATE}}$$

Figure 5 shows that failure to include X_2 in the extrapolation model leads to biased estimates of *PATE*. The magnitude of the bias depends on the in-sample correlation between X_1 and X_2. Strikingly, whenever $\rho > 0$, the *SATE* is closer to the true PATE than the estimate $\widehat{PATE}$.[32]

To understand where this bias comes from, consider first the case when $\rho = 1$, so $X_1 = X_2$ in-sample. Here, the sample conditional average treatment effect (CATE) corresponds to the sample CATEs for $X_2 \in \{0, 1\}$, but then we reweight by the population shares of $X_1 \in \{0, 1\}$. Since $X_1 = 1$ is rarer in the population than $X_2 = 1$, this leads to an *underestimate* of the PATE. A parallel logic holds for the case when $X_1 = 1 - X_2$ (when $\rho = -1$) in the sample. When $\rho = 0$, X_1 is independent of X_2 in the sample, then the CATEs for $X_1 \in \{0, 1\}$ are both equivalent to the SATE. When we evaluate the weighted average according to population shares of X_1, we (trivially) recover the PATE.

This simple example illustrates several limits of extrapolation-based approaches when recovering a PATE from the SATE. First, these approaches

---

[32] The negative relationship between ρ and PATE is stylized to our example.

rely on our ability to select covariates prognostic of (1) selection from the population into the experimental sample, and (2) treatment effect heterogeneity. The example shows that these models are susceptible to omitted variable bias whenever we do not know or cannot measure relevant covariates. Importantly, the set of covariates necessary to satisfy #1 and #2 may be different. Extrapolation-based approaches can provide unbiased estimation of the PATE only when (1) all relevant covariates can be identified and measured and (2) for each covariate profile, the probability of selection into the sample is neither zero nor one.[33]

Attentive readers should see the parallels between this discussion and the criticisms of our inability to reliably model selection into treatment that motivated the credibility revolution in the first place (e.g., Leamer, 1983). In this sense, recent developments in estimators to extrapolate the PATE from the SATE stand at odds with two of the three tenants of the credibility revolution that we describe in Chapter 1. Specifically, these methods rely on a model of the external world (data-generating process) governing both selection and treatment effect heterogeneity, rather than any research design. Moreover, when the aforementioned models are misspecified, as in our example, estimates of the PATE are susceptible to an unknowable amount of bias.

7.5 Application

Suppose that a watchdog organization or good governance-focused NGO in Brazil sought to implement the Brazilian electoral information intervention at scale. They may be worried that the sampling of participants and municipalities in the present experiment does not provide an estimate of the target intent-to-treat effect of the intervention because the participants differ on observables from the population of (voting-age) Pernambuco residents or Brazilians. The partner hypothesizes that treatment effects may vary on observable attributes, but that conditional on these attributes, treatment effects will not vary with the scale of administration or time. Specifically, they are worried that the experimental sample may not be representative of the adult population of Pernambuco or Brazil on the basis of gender, educational attainment, or age. While it is true that the experimental population is more male, less educated, and has a slightly different age distribution than either of the populations of interest, Figure 6 reveals that these compositional differences are not large.

Under our assumption of exact external validity, we can specify the mapping from (each) PATE to the observed SATE. Using this mapping, we use a reweighting-based estimator of the PATE to estimate both PATEs from

---

[33] The latter is known as a common support assumption and can be very strong under some conceptualizations of a population of interest.

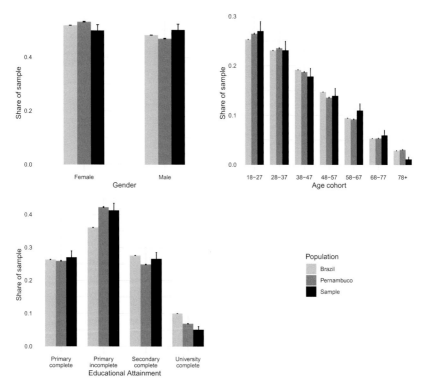

Figure 6 Comparison of experimental sample to all adult Brazilians and all adult Pernambuco residents on the basis of gender, educational attainment, and age. Intervals are 95% confidence intervals. Data for the Brazil and Pernambuco populations come from census microdata from 2010 from IPUMs.

the SATE. Our estimator is unbiased when sampling is ignorable, which we cannot know in this example. Figure 7 shows that the SATE and PATEs are very similar in magnitude and sign; all are very close to zero. This is predictable from Figure 6 since we can see that the marginal distributions of the three covariates across the three populations do not vary substantially.

Existing literature suggests that it may be more useful to estimate PATEs, or evaluate the difference between SATEs and PATEs, when the SATE is distinguishable from zero. For example, Devaux and Egami (2022) advocate for *external robustness*, which is the degree to which a population would have to differ from a sample for the SATE and the PATE to have different signs.[34] In our case, small perturbations in the population could easily flip the negative sign of

---

[34] Devaux and Egami (2022) refer to the PATE as the T-PATE, which stands for the target population average treatment effect.

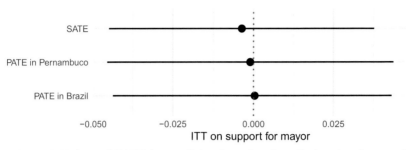

Figure 7 Estimated SATE (unconditional on signal quality) and estimates of
PATEs for all adults in Brazil and in the state of Pernambuco.

the SATE. But for our accountability example, it is reassuring to see a SATE and
PATEs near zero when we do not condition on the signal. This is consistent with
a population of voters whose prior beliefs (whether common or heterogeneous)
are not systematically biased. Of course, there are other plausible explanations
for the near-zero (unconditional) ITTs which we cannot eliminate.

It is worth pointing out the difference in this analysis compared to those of
the preceding sections. Here, we needed only one study to conduct this extrapolation exercise. We have not discussed the Mexico experiment, hence we have
omitted discussion of the cross-study environment. We made an assumption of
how effects would "transport" from subjects in the experimental municipalities
to the voting-age population in Pernambuco or in all of Brazil. Extrapolation
methods cannot be used to learn about external validity because external validity is "baked into" the extrapolation model. Such methods also abstract from
discussion about whether the same design would be plausible if the population
were changed. For example, could the same intervention be implemented at
scale in Brazil with an infinite budget? Would the higher saturation of treatment
change effects? If budgets were finite – as they typically are – what aspects
of the design would have to be changed to scale up the informational treatments? Extrapolation-based approaches typically abstract from these questions
entirely, even though they are central to the use of extrapolated estimates.

7.6 Extrapolation versus the Accumulation of Evidence

Extrapolation has gained prominence as an approach to questions related to
external validity. Conducting meta-studies has substantial costs in terms of
time, effort, and resources. Moreover, it is sometimes infeasible to conduct
a new study in a setting that may be important for characterizing the generality of a mechanism. For example, we cannot run new experiments in

historical settings. Extrapolation is feasible with data from a single study, and the covariates characterizing a population/setting of interest. We show that extrapolation does not permit inferences about potential empirical targets or estimates in other populations/settings, or their external validity, because they *assume* a structural model of the cross-study environment, including some form of a mechanism's external validity. These methods can answer questions, conditional on the assumed mapping between a source and destination.

Methodologists and practitioners who develop, or plan to use, extrapolation methods for making inferences about populations/settings outside of their sample (or the population sampled) should be aware of the tensions between the desire to pursue design-based methods for identification within study, and the model-based strategies used for extrapolation at the meta-study level. Given the speculative nature of the outputs from extrapolation exercises, they cannot be a substitute for actually measuring treatment effects in new settings. Consequently, *extrapolation is not a substitute for the accumulation of evidence*.

8 Conclusion

The scientific approach plays an important role in classifying, organizing, and most importantly, understanding social phenomena. A critical component of this approach is the ambition to study *general* social phenomena that transcend the circumstances in which they were observed and measured. In line with this aim, mechanisms occupy an increasingly important focus in the social sciences. Specifically, applied methodology emphasizes the measurement of the effects of (causal) mechanisms. This focus on mechanisms naturally gives rise to concerns about external validity and the development of methods to evaluate whether mechanisms possess such qualities.

We have outlined some of the most important theoretical concerns relevant to draw conclusions about general social phenomena from an empirical perspective. We focus on forms of empirical inquiry that are quantitative and our analysis explores the features of a study that allow one to draw quantitative conclusions from meta-studies. We provide a general framework, and a set of concepts, to synthesize, organize, and select among different approaches to evidence accumulation.

Our theoretical contribution is best summarized by four key takeaways:

1. An interest in general social phenomena belies an interest in mechanisms.
2. When studying a mechanism empirically, it is critical to consider how its influence is defined, assessed, and measured.

3. Any empirical approach that assesses the generality of social phenomena necessarily engages with external validity, and there are multiple ways to formulate it.
4. Any approach to evidence accumulation must articulate **uniting principles**.

Uniting principles are critical for evidence accumulation because they connect or unite different constituent studies. Quantitative approaches to evidence accumulation require uniting principles that provide a theoretical basis for a *quantitative relationship between constituent studies*. The first uniting principle, common concepts, is about formulating a qualitative conceptual link between different studies and is widely appreciated. Uniting Principle II, quantitative connection, is less appreciated but just as important. It specifies the quantitative relationship between studies and is needed for a meta-study's results to have any quantitative meaning or interpretation.

We apply our theoretical concepts to assess the two most common applications of evidence accumulation – meta-analysis and replication – as well as the principal alternative to evidence accumulation: extrapolation. We show how each approach fulfills the two uniting principles. Our analysis reveals how each approach engages with distinct formulations of external validity. We show that prominent applications of meta-analysis, which rely on hierarchical models of the cross-study environment, typically beg the question of external validity. Consequently, they cannot conclude anything about external validity since it is an underlying assumption of the meta-analytic model (e.g., the fixed- and random-effects models). Replication, on the other hand, can be used to assess external validity, but only when specific features of the constituent studies (harmonization) are satisfied. These features of meta-study design are often taken for granted. Finally, extrapolation approaches use various structural models to "predict" or "impute" effects elsewhere. Extrapolation-based approaches rely on some formulation of external validity to justify the exercise. The strong assumptions that underpin extrapolation approaches typically abandon the most important tenants of the credibility revolution, such as the elimination of bias.

Evidence accumulation is often advocated as the next step in the continued progress of the social sciences. We conclude with several imperatives for a continuing research agenda on evidence accumulation. First, our measurement perspectivist view of empirical research and measurement stresses the need to understand the relationship between the research designs that are used in constituent studies and evidence accumulation efforts. Second, understanding the promise and limits of design-based strategies to the accumulation of evidence – both in terms of what can be learned and what must be assumed given a set of uniting principles – allows for reflection on design-based and structural approaches to evidence accumulation.

Finally, we point to a tendency among practitioners to stress the importance of design-based identification strategies at the single-study level, but then advocate for elaborate model-based strategies for evidence accumulation. This tension deserves more attention. If the lessons and principles of the credibility revolution are unnecessary – or too stringent – as scholars try to generalize their empirical findings, should the importance of identification and bias at the single-study level be re-evaluated? If not, future work that aims to isolate, measure, and understand the influence of general social mechanisms, and draw conclusions that are broader than just the individual studies that measure a constituent-level effect, need to adopt design-based approaches to meta-studies. By doing so, inferences obtained from exercises in evidence accumulation can preserve the kind of credibility of causal inferences that is so highly valued at the level of individual studies.

References

Allcott, H. (2015). Site selection bias in program evaluation. *The Quarterly Journal of Economics*, *130*(3), 1117–1165.

Andrews, I., & Oster, E. (2019). A simple approximation for evaluating external validity bias. *Economics Letters*, *178*, 58–62.

Angrist, J. D., & Pischke, J.- S. (2008). *Mostly harmless econometrics: An empiricist's companion*. Princeton University Press.

Angrist, J. D., & Pischke, J.- S. (2010). The credibility revolution in empirical economics: How better research design is taking the con out of econometrics. *Journal of Economic Perspectives*, *24*(2), 3–30.

Arias, E., Larreguy, H., Marshall, J., & Querubin, P. (2022). Priors rule: When do malfeasance revelations help or hurt incumbent parties? *Journal of the European Economic Association*, *20*(4), 1433–1477.

Aronow, P. M., & Miller, B. T. (2019). *Foundations of agnostic statistics*. Cambridge University Press.

Ashworth, S. (2012). Electoral accountability: Recent theoretical and empirical work. *Annual Review of Political Science*, *15*(1), 183–201.

Ashworth, S., Berry, C. R., & de Mesquita, E. B. (2021). *Theory and credibility: Integrating theoretical and empirical social science*. Princeton University Press.

Ashworth, S., Bueno de Mesquita, E., & Friedenberg, A. (2018). Learning about voter rationality. *American Journal of Political Science*, *62*(1), 37–54.

Banerjee, A., & Duflo, E. (2009). The experimental approach to development economics. *Annual Review of Economics*, *1*, 151–178.

Banerjee, A., Duflo, E., Goldberg, N., et al. (2015). A multifaceted program causes lasting progress for the very poor: Evidence from six countries. *Science*, *348*(6236), 1–17.

Berger, R. L. (1982). Multiparameter hypothesis testing and acceptance sampling. *Technometrics*, *24*(4), 295–300.

Besley, T. (2006). *Principled agents?: The political economy of good government*. Oxford University Press.

Björkman, M., & Svensson, J. (2009). Power to the people: Evidence from a randomized field experiment on community-based monitoring in Uganda. *The Quarterly Journal of Economics*, *124*(2), 735–769.

Blair, G., Cooper, J., Coppock, A., & Humphreys, M. (2019). Declaring and diagnosing research designs. *American Political Science Review*, *113*(3), 838–859.

Blair, G., Weinstein, J. M., Christia, F., et al. (2021). Community policing does not build citizen trust in police or reduce crime in the global south. *Science*, *374*(6571), eabd3446.

Boas, T. C., Hidalgo, F., & Melo, M. (2019). Norms versus action: Why voters fail to sanction malfeasance in Brazil. *American Journal of Political Science*, *63*(2), 385–400.

Bogen, J., & Woodward, J. (1988). Saving the phenomena. *The Philosophical Review*, *97*(3), 303–352.

Borsboom, D. (2005). *Measuring the mind: Conceptual issues in contemporary psychometrics*. Cambridge University Press.

Brinch, C. N., Mogstad, M., & Wiswall, M. (2017). Beyond LATE with a discrete instrument. *Journal of Political Economy*, *125*(4), 985–1039.

Brodeur, A., Cook, N., & Heyes, A. (2020). Methods matter: P-hacking and publication bias in causal analysis in economics. *American Economic Review*, *110*(11), 3634–3600.

Bueno de Mesquita, E., & Tyson, S. A. (2020). The commensurability problem: Conceptual difficulties in estimating the effect of behavior on behavior. *American Political Science Review*, *114*(2), 375–391.

Camerer, C. F., Dreber, A., Forsell, E., et al. (2016). Evaluating replicability of laboratory experiments in economics. *Science*, *351*(6280), 1433–1436.

Camerer, C. F., Dreber, A., Holzmeister, F., et al. (2018). Evaluating the replicability of social science experiments in nature and science between 2010 and 2015. *Nature Human Behaviour*, *2*(9), 637–644.

Chakravartty, A. (2007). *A metaphysics for scientific realism: Knowing the unobservable*. Cambridge University Press.

Chang, H. (2001). Spirit, air, and quicksilver: The search for the "real" scale of temperature. *Historical Studies in the Physical and Biological Sciences*, *31*(2), 249–284.

Chang, H. (2004). *Inventing temperature: Measurement and scientific progress*. Oxford University Press.

Cheung, M. W.- L. (2014). Modeling dependent effect sizes with three-level meta-analyses: A structural equation modeling approach. *Psychological Methods*, *19*(2), 211.

Chong, A., de la O, A., Karlan, D., & Wantchekon, L. (2015). Quash the hope? A field experiment in Mexico on voter turnout, choice, and party identification. *Journal of Politics, 77*(1), 55–71.

Clayton, A., O'Brien, D., & Piscopo, J. M. (2019). All male panels? Representation and democratic legitimacy. *American Journal of Political Science*, *63*(1), 113–129.

Cole, S. R., & Stuart, E. A. (2010). Generalizing evidence from randomized clinical trials to target populations: The actg 320 trial. *American Journal of Epidemiology*, *172*(1), 107–115.

Collins, H. (1992). *Changing order: Replication and induction in scientific practice*. University of Chicago Press.

Coppock, A., Hill, S. J., & Vavreck, L. (2020). The small effects of political advertising are small regardless of context, message, sender, or receiver: Evidence from 59 real-time randomized experiments. *Science Advances*, *6*(eabc4046), 1–6.

de la O, A., Green, D. P., John, P., et al. (2021). Fiscal contracts? A six-country randomized experiment on transaction costs, public services, and taxation in developing countries. *Working paper*. https://nikhargaikwad.com/resources/De-La-O-et-al_2021.pdf

Dear, P. (1995). *Discipline and experience: The mathematical way in the scientific revolution*. University of Chicago Press.

Deaton, A. (2010). Instruments, randomization, and learning about development. *Journal of Economic Literature*, *48*(2), 424–455.

Deaton, A., & Cartwright, N. (2018). Understanding and misunderstanding randomized controlled trials. *Social Science & Medicine*, *210*, 2–21.

Dehejia, R., Pop-Eleches, C., & Samii, C. (2021). From local to global: External validity in a fertility natural experiment. *Journal of Business & Economic Statistics*, *39*(1), 217–243.

Devaux, M., & Egami, N. (2022, September). *Quantifying robustness to external validity bias*. (Working paper available at https://naokiegami.com/paper/external_robust.pdf)

Diaconis, P., & Skyrms, B. (2017). *Ten great ideas about chance*. Princeton University Press.

Dunning, T. (2016). Transparency, replication, and cumulative learning: What experiments alone cannot achieve. *Annual Review of Political Science*, *19*, 541–563.

Dunning, T., Grossman, G., Humphreys, M., et al. (2019a). Voter information campaigns and political accountability: Cumulative findings from a preregistered meta-analysis of coordinated trials. *Science Advances*, *5*(7), 1–10.

Dunning, T., Grossman, G., Humphreys, M., et al. (Eds.). (2019b). *Information, accountability, and cumulative learning: Lessons from Metaketa I*. Cambridge University Press.

Egami, N., & Hartman, E. (2023). Elements of external validity: Framework, design, and analysis. *American Political Science Review*, *117*(3), 1070–1088.

Fariss, C. J., & Jones, Z. M. (2018). Enhancing validity in observational settings when replication is not possible. *Political Science Research and Methods*, *6*(2), 365–380.

Ferejohn, J. (1986). Incumbent performance and electoral control. *Public Choice*, *50*, 5–25.

Findley, M. G., Kikuta, K., & Denly, M. (2021). External validity. *Annual Review of Political Science*, *24*, 365–393.

Fowler, A., & Montagnes, B. P. (2023). Distinguishing between false positives and genuine results: The case of irrelevant events and elections. *The Journal of Politics*, *85*(1), 304–309.

Gailmard, S. (2021). Theory, history, and political economy. *Journal of Historical Political Economy*, *1*(1), 69–104.

Gechter, M., & Meager, R. (2021). Combining experimental and observational studies in meta-analysis: A mutual debiasing approach.*Mimeo*. www.personal.psu.edu/mdg5396/MGRM_Combining_Experimental_and_Observational_Studies.pdf

Gerber, A. S., & Green, D. P. (2012). *Field experiments: Design, analysis and interpretation*. W. W. Norton.

Gerber, A. S., & Malhotra, N. (2008). Do statistical reporting standards affect what is Published? Publication bias in two leading political science journals. *Quarterly Journal of Political Science*, *3*(3), 313–326.

Giere, R. N. (2010). *Scientific perspectivism*. University of Chicago press.

Glennan, S. (1996). Mechanisms and the nature of causation. *Erkenntnis*, *44*(1), 49–71.

Glennan, S. (2017). *The new mechanical philosophy*. Oxford University Press.

Godefroidt, A. (2023). How terrorism does (and does not) affect citizens' political attitudes: A meta-analysis. *American Journal of Political Science*, *67*(1), 22–38.

Graham, M. H., Huber, G. A., Malhotra, N., & Mo, C. H. (2023). How should we think about replicating observational studies? A reply to Fowler and Montagnes. *The Journal of Politics*, *85*(1), 310–313.

Guala, F. (2003). Experimental localism and external validity. *Philosophy of Science*, *70*(5), 1195–1205.

Guala, F. (2005). *The methodology of experimental economics*. Cambridge University Press.

Hacking, I. (1983). *Representing and intervening: Introductory topics in the philosophy of natural science*. Cambridge university press.

Hamming, R. W. (1980). The unreasonable effectiveness of mathematics. *The American Mathematical Monthly*, *87*(2), 81–90.

Hartman, E., & Hidalgo, F. (2018). An equivalence approach to balance and placebo tests. *American Journal of Political Science, 62*(4), 1000–1013.

Heckman, J. J., & Vytlacil, E. (2005). Structural equations, treatment effects, and econometric policy evaluation 1. *Econometrica, 73*(3), 669–738.

Huber, J. D. (2017). *Exclusion by elections: Inequality, ethnic identity, and democracy*. Cambridge University Press.

Hume, D. (1777). *Enquiries concerning the human understanding and concerning the principles of morals*. Oxford University Press.

Imbens, G. W., & Wooldridge, J. M. (2009). Recent developments in the econometrics of program evaluation. *Journal of Economic Literature, 47*(1), 5–86.

Incerti, T. (2020). Corruption information and vote share: A meta-analysis and lessons for experimental design. *American Political Science Review, 114*(3), 761–774.

Izzo, F., Dewan, T., & Wolton, S. (2022). Cumulative knowledge in the social sciences: The case of improving voters' information. *Available at SSRN 3239047*.

Jerven, M. (2013). *Poor numbers*. Cornell University Press.

Kern, H. L., Stuart, E. A., Hill, J., & Green, D. P. (2016). Assessing methods for generalizing experimental impact estimates to target populations. *Journal of Research on Educational Effectiveness, 9*, 103–127.

Latour, B. (1993). *The pasteurization of France*. Harvard University Press.

Latour, B., & Woolgar, S. (1986). *Laboratory life: The construction of scientific facts*. Princeton University Press.

Leamer, E. E. (1983). Let's take the con out of econometrics. *The American Economic Review, 73*(1), 31–43.

Leibniz, G. W. (1714). The monadology. In Jonathan C. W. Edwards (Ed.) *Philosophical papers and letters* (pp. 643–653). Springer 1989.

Mares, I., & Visconti, G. (2020). Voting for the lesser evil: Evidence from a conjoint experiment in Romania. *Political Science Research and Methods, 8*, 315–328.

Marquis de Laplace, P. S. (1825). *A philosophical essay on probabilities*. Wiley 1902.

Mayo, D. G. (1996). *Error and the growth of experimental knowledge*. University of Chicago Press.

Meager, R. (2019). Understanding the average impact of microcredit expansions: A Bayesian hierarchical analysis of seven randomized experiments. *American Economic Journal: Applied Economics, 11*(1), 57–91.

Mill, J. S. (1856). *A system of logic, ratiocinative and inductive: 1* (Vol. 1). Parker.

Moher, D., Shamseer, L., Clarke, M., et al. (2015). Preferred reporting items for systematic review and meta-analysis (prisma-p) 2015 statement. *Systematic Reviews*, *4*(1), 1–9.

Munger, K. (2023). Temporal validity as meta-science. *Research & Politics*, *10*(3), 20531680231187271.

Open Science Collaboration. (2015). Estimating the reproducibility of psychological science. *Science*, *349*(6251), 1–8.

Orzack, S. H., & Sober, E. (1993). A critical assessment of Levins's The strategy of model building in population biology (1966). *The Quarterly Review of Biology*, *68*(4), 533–546.

Pearl, J., & Bareinboim, E. (2011). Transportability of causal and statistical relations: A formal approach. In *Twenty-fifth AAAI conference on artificial intelligence.*

Pearl, J., & Bareinboim, E. (2014). External validity: From do-calculus to transportability across populations. *Statistical Science*, *29*(4), 579–595.

Pritchett, L., & Sandefur, J. (2015). Learning from experiments when context matters. *American Economic Review*, *105*(5), 471–475.

Putnam, H. (1981). *Reason, truth and history*. Cambridge University Press.

Raffler, P., Posner, D. N., & Parkerson, D. (2020, October). *Can citizen pressure be induced to improve public service provision?* (Working paper, Harvard University)

Salmon, W. C. (1984). *Scientific explanation and the causal structure of the world*. Princeton University Press.

Samii, C. (2016). Causal empiricism in quantitative research. *The Journal of Politics*, *78*(3), 941–955.

Schedler, A. (2012). Judgment and measurement in political science. *Perspectives on Politics*, *10*(1), 21–36.

Schwarz, S., & Coppock, A. (2022). What have we learned about gender from candidate choice experiments? A meta-analysis of 67 factorial survey experiments. *Journal of Politics*, *84*(2), 655–668.

Shadish, W., Cook, T. D., & Campbell, D. T. (2002). *Experimental and quasi-experimental designs for generalized causal inference*. Houghton Mifflin.

Slough, T. (2024). Bureaucratic quality and electoral accountability. *American Political Science Review, Forthcoming.*

Slough, T., Rubenson, D., Levy, R., et al. (2021). Adoption of community monitoring improves common pool resource management across contexts. *Proceedings of the National Academy of Sciences*, *10*(1073), 1–10.

Slough, T., & Tyson, S. A. (2023). External validity and meta-analysis. *American Journal of Political Science*, *67*(2), 440–455.

Slough, T., & Tyson, S. A. (2024). Sign-congruent external validity and replication. Political Analysis, Forthcoming.

Smith, V. L. (1982). Microeconomic systems as an experimental science. *The American Economic Review*, *72*(5), 923–955.

Venn, J. (1888). *The logic of chance: An essay on the foundations and province of the theory of probability, with especial reference to its logical bearings and its application to moral and social science, and to statistics*. Macmillan.

Woodward, J. (2002). What is a mechanism? A counterfactual account. *Philosophy of Science*, *69*(S3), S366–S377.

Acknowledgments

We thank Sean Gailmard and participants at the Uses of Formal Theory Conference at the University of Chicago for comments on an early version of this Element. Jessica Sun provided insightful comments on a later version of the manuscript. This Element builds upon two earlier papers that were greatly improved by comments from Scott Abramson, P. M. Aronow, Neal Beck, Kevin Clarke, Alex Coppock, Chris Fariss, Don Green, Guy Grossman, Federica Izzo, Gleason Judd, Dorothy Kronick, Winston Lin, John Marshall, Walter Mebane, Francesca Molinari, Kevin Munger, John Patty, Dan Posner, Pablo Querubín, Pia Raffler, Mark Ratkovic, Cyrus Samii, Jessica Sun, Ian Turner, Ed Vytlacil, Anna Wilke, Stephane Wolton, Hye Young You, and anonymous reviewers. We are grateful for Neal Beck's encouragement to write this Element.

Cambridge Elements ☰

Quantitative and Computational Methods for the Social Sciences

R. Michael Alvarez
California Institute of Technology

R. Michael Alvarez has taught at the California Institute of Technology his entire career, focusing on elections, voting behavior, election technology, and research methodologies. He has written or edited a number of books (recently, *Computational Social Science: Discovery and Prediction*, and *Evaluating Elections: A Handbook of Methods and Standards*) and numerous academic articles and reports.

Nathaniel Beck
New York University

Nathaniel Beck is Professor of Politics at NYU (and Affiliated Faculty at the NYU Center for Data Science) where he has been since 2003, before which he was Professor of Political Science at the University of California, San Diego. He is the founding editor of the quarterly, *Political Analysis*. He is a fellow of both the American Academy of Arts and Sciences and the Society for Political Methodology.

Betsy Sinclair
Washington University in St. Louis

Betsy Sinclair is Professor and Chair of Political Science at WashU. Her research focuses on social influence and American political behavior. She is a fellow of the Society of Political Methodology and has served as an associate editor of Political Analysis and in leadership roles in The Society of Political Methodology and Visions in Political Methodology.

About the Series

The Elements Series Quantitative and Computational Methods for the Social Sciences contains short introductions and hands-on tutorials to innovative methodologies. These are often so new that they have no textbook treatment or no detailed treatment on how the method is used in practice. Among emerging areas of interest for social scientists, the series presents machine learning methods, the use of new technologies for the collection of data and new techniques for assessing causality with experimental and quasi-experimental data.

Cambridge Elements ☰

Quantitative and Computational Methods for the Social Sciences